RESTORING THE FALLEN

A Team Approach to Caring, Confronting & Reconciling

Earl & Sandy Wilson
Paul & Virginia Friesen
Larry & Nancy Paulson

InterVarsity Press
Downers Grove, Illinois

InterVarsity Press® is the book-publishing division of InterVarsity Christian Fellowship®, a student movement active on campus at hundreds of universities, colleges and schools of nursing in the United States of America, and a member movement of the International Fellowship of Evangelical Students. For information about local and regional activities, write Public Relations Dept., InterVarsity Christian Fellowship, 6400 Schroeder Rd., P.O. Box 7895, Madison, WI 53707-7895.

All Scripture quotations, unless otherwise indicated, are taken from the HOLY BIBLE, NEW INTERNATIONAL VERSION® NIV® Copyright ©1973, 1978, 1984 by International Bible Society. Used by permission of Zondervan Publishing House. All rights reserved.

ISBN 0-8308-1619-4

Printed in the United States of America ∞

Library of Congress Cataloging-in-Publication Data

Restoring the fallen: a team approach to caring, confronting &
    reconciling/Earl and Sandra Wilson . . . [et al.].
        p.   cm.
    Includes bibliographical references.
    ISBN 0-8308-1619-4 (pbk.: alk. paper)
    1. Church discipline.   2. Church group work.   3. Repentance—
Christianity.   4. Reconciliation—Religious aspects—Christianity.
I. Wilson, Earl D., 1939-   .
BV740.R47   1996
253'.7—dc20   96-2808
                                                                              CIP

| 19 | 18 | 17 | 16 | 15 | 14 | 13 | 12 | 11 | 10 | 9 | 8 | 7 | 6 | 5 | 4 | 3 | 2 | 1 |

| 12 | 11 | 10 | 09 | 08 | 07 | 06 | 05 | 04 | 03 | 02 | 01 | 00 | 99 | 98 | 97 |

RESTORING THE FALLEN

A Team Approach to Caring, Confronting & Reconciling

Earl & Sandy Wilson

Paul & Virginia Friesen

Larry & Nancy Paulson

To our children:
Marcie, Mark, Michael, Melissa, Mickey
Kari, Lisa, Julie
Duke, Scott, Bryce

May God give you opportunities to be care-givers
to those in need, and, as needed,
may he provide those who will care for you.

Preface

This book has six authors. But we are really a single author, since we are a team and the experience we went through together is the basis for this book.

Much of the story is told by Earl Wilson. A therapist and writer who helped others with their personal struggles, he did not deal with his own secret problem: sexual addiction. But his secret finally came out, and Earl was forced to ask for help. Paul and Virginia Friesen, experienced in counseling couples, and church friends Larry and Nancy Paulson joined Earl and his wife, Sandy, as a Spiritual Care Team, together helping to restore the lives and ministry shattered by Earl's sin. The team worked in consultation with Earl's therapist, Dr. Daniel McIvor. For all other people mentioned in the stories in this book, names and circumstances have been changed to protect privacy.

Throughout the book you will hear the others' voices at certain points, and Sandy writes a chapter from the viewpoint of the spouse. All the principles we suggest were learned by our team through the intense and difficult experience that began in the fall of 1989.

As you read the book, we trust you will find a thread running through all the chapters: *the importance of honesty in all our relationships.* Honesty with ourselves, God, spouse, children, church and friends. This book is not only the story of a man caught in sexual sin and restored; it is also a challenge to every Christian to live in honesty and truth. It could be subtitled "one man's journey from image to reality, from falsehood to truthfulness, from distance to intimacy." As you read, don't be surprised if you are faced with your own issues of honesty in relationships.

Earl thought his life was over. But with God's help, restoration has been achieved—moral, emotional, professional, marital and spiritual. The team has written this book with gratitude to the Great Physician and Wonderful Counselor who guided and strengthened us throughout the process. It is our hope that many broken persons will dare to reach out for help, find a Spiritual Care Team and with them go through the process of finding full restoration.

1

The Day the Roof Fell In

It was late when we arrived home from the football game. Sandy, my wife, and I were both surprised when we were greeted by our daughter. "Welcome home," she said. "How was the game?" Before we could answer, she said, "Oh! By the way, Dad, there's a certified letter for you on the counter."

I went in and picked up the letter. I began to feel the grip of fear even before I could open it. The return address read "Board of Psychologist Examiners."

"What's that, honey?" my wife asked.

"Nothing," I replied, lying through my teeth. "It's some kind of complaint. I'm too tired to figure it out tonight; I'll study it in the morning."

We crawled into bed, and Sandy was soon fast asleep. Sleep did not come as easily to me, however. The letter I had gotten didn't describe "some kind of complaint." It revealed in accurate detail an ethical violation that I had lied about, denied, misrepresented and covered up. The letter stated that I, as a licensed psychologist, had prematurely terminated treatment of a client and then had engaged in a sexual relationship with that client. I was desperate to try and cover up and justify my behavior and to escape the inevitable pain about to engulf me, my wife and my family. I realized that God's Word is certainly true when it says, "A man reaps what he sows" (Gal 6:7). My inner turmoil was boiling up into panic.

When we got up the next morning, I succeeded in avoiding the issue with Sandy for a while longer. We hurried to church, came home and ate lunch, and then I excused myself to take a walk. I was desperately searching for a way to talk to the woman who had filed the complaint and have her drop the allegations so that it would all go away. Confusion and despair overwhelmed me.

Meanwhile, Sandy suspected that something was up. *This is strange,* she thought. *What could be going on? He's been gone for a long time. What about that letter? Could that be what's bothering him?* She found the letter and read it quickly. Her worst fears were confirmed. *So he did have sex with her. I thought so all along. What does this mean to us now? our marriage? our family?* Sandy struggled to keep from being overwhelmed by anger and betrayal as a million thoughts rushed through her mind.

I returned home from my walk, and we began to talk. Not knowing that Sandy had seen the letter, I related the details of the complaint to her and admitted for the first time that I had committed physical adultery.

Years earlier I had become sexually involved with this former client. When Sandy had become aware of my personal involvement with this woman, I had convinced her that it had been only an intense emotional relationship and not a physical one. I had also led Sandy to believe that I had terminated all contact with the woman. None of this was true. Although the relationship had not involved sexual intercourse for a number of years, I had secretly maintained regular contact with her.

I was not just an adulterer; I was also a liar. All my sins were now lying at my doorstep in the full light of day. It was not just the roof that fell in on me—the walls caved in as well.

In the life of every church there are times when individuals or families have spiritual needs that go beyond the scope of care usually provided by the church. An elder may confess that he has cheated on his wife, a pastor may confess (or be caught) to having a sexual affair with a parishioner, or an assistant leader in the youth program may be arrested for driving while intoxicated. Our story represents the pain many Christians experience during an intense crisis. In all of these examples faith is challenged, sins must be dealt with, and a recovery and restoration process will have to be started. In situation after situation churches find themselves needing to do something but not knowing what to do. There seems to be a dearth of good models to follow that can help people express and deal with the intense emotional and spiritual needs that arise.

The purpose of this book is to present one such model, the Spiritual Care Team, and to describe how it can be implemented in a variety of situations. The model will be presented in a case-study format using our story, with additional stories from other people's situations.

What Is a Spiritual Care Team?

Sometimes a serious physical illness can land us in the hospital's intensive care unit (or ICU). A Spiritual Care Team is another kind of ICU. It is a group of mature Christians who voluntarily commit themselves to support and assist a person or persons with acute spiritual needs through a process of returning that person to fellowship with God, family and fellow believers.

When there is a crisis, the persons involved need targeted, intensive attention to ensure that spiritual fatalities do not occur. The church has been accused, sometimes rightly, of shooting its wounded and abandoning those whose behavior is less than exemplary. Could it be that we, as the church, have not known what to do? Have we excused ourselves and failed to act responsibly toward those who have committed grievous sins but need our help?

The Spiritual Care Team model presented in this book uses the example of a team formed after a Christian leader had been caught in sexual sin. It is not, however, a book just about restoration of Christian leaders or just about sexual sin. Any believer who turns from God to any kind of sin is in need of restoration. The principles presented here are applicable to a wide range of people and situations.

This book is a practical discussion of the process of restoration. It is not intended to be as much a how-to manual as a challenge or call to action. The material is presented with three thoughts in mind:

1. to bring hope to those who are broken or disillusioned and in need of restoration

2. to provide guidance and direction for those seeking to help shattered individuals or families

3. to encourage honesty as we relate to one another

Our goal is to encourage a ministry of restoration that incorporates discipline, accountability and compassion. This biblically based ministry has historically been severely neglected in the church. This book articulates a serious challenge: to be actively and positively involved in someone's life. Our story suggests how the Christian community is able to come alongside fallen brothers and sisters and restore them fully—to a life of fellowship with God, to wholeness in their family and to usefulness in the Christian community.

Toward a More Effective Approach

Galatians 6:1 tells us, "Brothers, if someone is caught in a sin, you who are spiritual should restore him gently. But watch yourself, or you also may be tempted." As Christians we are therefore supposed to restore fellow sinners—but we do not always know *how* to restore.

Efforts to achieve restoration are often inadequate or unbiblical. In many cases, restoration is nonexistent. We believe that the model shown in this book is not only biblically based but practical and applicable to the local church.

There are three common approaches to dealing with Christians who have fallen into sin.

1. Cast the sinner out. With this mindset we react with shock that any genuine Christian could have committed such a sin. The "righteous" remove sinners from the congregation and suggest they not return to the church or make it extremely uncomfortable for them to do so. This method attempts to deal swiftly with the problem so life can go on. It may serve the immediate purpose of getting things "back to normal" in the church, but it lacks any expression of care for the offender or others who have been hurt by the sin.

Those who advocate this method will cite the swift acts of judgment in Scripture in order to "maintain a pure remnant." Eliminating people without effort to restore them, however, is a distortion of this biblical principle. The church is weakened by any response that demonstrates a lack of understanding of the biblical mandate to be involved in bringing a person back into fellowship through the process of *restoration and discipline* along with the application of *mercy and grace.*

2. Ignore the sin, pretending it never happened. Denial is the second method practiced by some congregations, ignoring the sin and acting as if it had never happened. People know about the sin but choose not to confront the sinner. We justify our lack of

involvement with statements like
☐ "When you point one finger at someone, three fingers will be pointing back at you."
☐ "The loving thing is not to make the sinning person feel awkward about this."
☐ "If I bring this up, others will think I'm critical."
☐ "The less attention the better."
☐ "If you ignore the sin, it will go away."
☐ "Who am I to judge?"

In Matthew 7:1-5 Jesus addresses the issue of judging each other. His emphasis, however, is not on overlooking sin or refusing to confront others' sin. He is pointing out that *hypocritical* judgment of sin is not acceptable. We are not to talk about the speck in a fellow believer's eye when we have a plank in our own. There is an important warning here. Those of us who follow Christ and seek to serve others must practice self-examination and self-judgment in order to guard our own lives. This prepares us to responsibly and carefully confront those who have chosen sinful paths. Jesus never encouraged us to ignore sin. He instead challenges us to live holy lives and to encourage others to do so.

3. Forgive and forget. The third common method of responding to sin is to encourage everyone to quickly "forgive and forget." If the sinner is "sorry," then he or she should be forgiven immediately and restored to the fellowship and to the position or responsibilities they were holding previously. This method boasts of extending mercy and grace. The "sorrowful" pastor who confesses adultery on Wednesday is able to be in the pulpit the following Sunday without any evidence of repentance or restoration. In other instances the so-called restoration process is completed within a matter of weeks or a few months. This quick-fix method has great appeal because it is what we would want if we were caught in our sin. (One pastor we know of defended his decision to hire a man accused of sexual sin by saying, "I'm treating him just as I would want to be treated if I were in his place.") But the quick fix distorts the reality that sin springs from deep within the heart and cannot be effectively dealt with in a superficial manner or brief time period.

The missing component in each of these commonly applied methods is true restoration: bringing a person back. True restoration is achieved through a process of discipline that recognizes both grace and responsibility as it seeks to guide the individual back to a God-centered life. Casting out doesn't make any provision for restoration. Denial ignores the problem and thus sees no need for the discipline process. The forgive-and-forget approach does not require action because restoration has been granted instantly. Is it any wonder that the church is so ineffective in dealing with sin in our midst when these are the approaches we are most often using?

The church is in desperate need of a biblically based model that deals with sin effectively. The model of restoration presented in the following chapters emphasizes four ideas:

1. the importance of dealing with the truth regarding sin
2. the need for complete repentance
3. the need for the establishment or reestablishment of spiritual principles and disciplines
4. the need for restoration of damaged relationships

Throughout this book, our story is presented along with principles and procedures that can be drawn from the restoration process. We share this story not to exploit it in any way but to flesh out the effectiveness of this model of handling restoration. We have seen that with God's help evil can be stopped and a person spiritually adrift can find the joy of a restored relationship with God and family.

2

Digging Out from the Rubble

*S**andy's initial response to** my revelation of adultery was shock mixed with compassion conditioned by years of unquestioning support and encouragement. She didn't allow her negative feelings to surface until later. I remember her saying, "We'll get through this." That was Sunday afternoon. She could have walked out, but she didn't.

We agreed that I should immediately talk to three people: my best friend, my business partner and an attorney. At this point I was not really facing the impact of what I had done. I was trying desperately to keep it at arm's length, as just a problem to be solved. I wasn't ready to take a look at myself or my behavior.

When I told my best friend, he expressed his concern and tried to help me calm down and think things through. I appreciated his loyalty and his willingness to listen to me and ask questions to clarify my thoughts and future steps. He didn't try to solve anything, but I knew he was there for me. His response comforted me but also made me aware that he was leaving the problem squarely in my lap, where it belonged.

As the week continued my thoughts ran rampant. How could I get out of this mess? My desire was for a quick and easy solution. I clearly did not want to face what I had done. I did not want my sins to have consequences. My focus was on my own pain. I could not let myself think of Sandy's pain; in fact, I couldn't even look her in the eye. My sins had dealt our relationship a tragic, possibly fatal, blow, but I could not and would not consider that. I was panicked only by thoughts of losing my career and reputation.

My conversations with my business partner were confusing to us both. I searched for assurances from him that our business and our friendship would not be affected. In a crazy attempt to prove to myself that things would be okay, I even planned an expansion of our business to the other side of the city. Within two weeks of my confession to him, however, he approached me with a different reality: he wanted to sever our partnership. I could hardly believe my ears. One of my worst fears was coming true: I was losing the business we had worked so hard to put together. Even though he assured me that we would always be friends and that he would never be in business with anyone else, I was painfully beginning to realize that things could never be the same. I was confused and hurt.

Although I asked him to reconsider, he remained firm, and I finally agreed to sell him my interest in the business. Our beautiful new suite of offices vanished in front of my eyes, and I was facing the possibility of losing my professional license as well. My hope that the revelation of my adultery would not interrupt my life was vanishing. The consequences of my sin were coming home to roost.

When I thought about hiring an attorney, Robert's name came to mind. I had always thought that if I were in trouble, I'd want him in my corner. I felt a false sense of comfort as I remembered this and made the telephone call. He was supportive, cordial and optimistic about my case. I think he was unknowingly supporting the deep denial in which I was entrenched. His approach fed my desire to believe that I really hadn't done anything too wrong. But God knew better.

Sandy had said on Sunday that she would stay with me and stand by me, but by the time we had dinner together on Thursday night, she said she was going to leave. I was devastated once more. Suddenly I was forced to consider the possibility of losing my wife and family as well as my career and ministry. I pleaded with Sandy not to go. She was scheduled to leave the next morning to speak at a women's conference, and she said she would try to think it over while she was gone. After she left, I was frightened and alone, clinging to a straw of hope. When she returned from the conference, she said she had decided to stay for now. I didn't know why she had changed her mind, and I was afraid to ask. My spirits were buoyed once more. Again I glossed over the possibility of losing her. My optimistic outlook rested in the expectation that it would all work out.

Sandy and I were scheduled the next weekend to conduct workshops at a large conference. It was too late to cancel, so we agreed we would do the best we could. We didn't deal with many of our issues that week; our focus was on getting ready for our workshops and day-to-day survival. Ironically, one of the workshop topics was intimacy in marriage. We both felt raw and exposed trying to minister to others when we needed desperately to be ministered to ourselves.

During the conference we stayed at a motel. This time alone provided us an opportunity to talk and to ponder our future. I was still looking for a quick fix, but Sandy was much more realistic, and it was she who first mentioned the need for additional help and guidance. She was wise enough to realize that we could not go on with life as usual; I still clung to the hope that we could. I was very deep in denial, unwilling to face the damage I had done or the hurt I had caused. I was selfishly trying to get rid of my pain and get on with life. At this point I wasn't looking for restoration; I was looking for an escape from the consequences of what I had done.

That weekend we sat on the bed in the motel wondering, "Where can we turn?" I still wanted to try to patch things up myself, but Sandy kept coming back to our need for someone to guide us. I was afraid, believing that the more people who knew, the more loss *I* would experience. Our church was without a senior pastor at the time, and Sandy and I were reluctant to go to the interim leaders for help. As we thought about possible resources to whom we could turn, Paul and Virginia Friesen came to mind. Our relationship with them had developed over the years through our speaking engagements at different InterVarsity camps that Paul supervised. Sandy and I made the decision that Paul and Virginia were the ones to whom we should turn.

I called Paul to see if they would have some time to meet with us. He asked what it was about. I remember avoiding the question and just saying, "I have a lot of confessing to do, so just have a big box of Kleenex on hand."

Paul recalls, "The conversation was marked by urgency and ambiguity. 'Paul, this is Earl. Could you and Virginia clear a weekend in your schedule so we could come down? It's important that we see you soon. It won't be a happy meeting.' Earl avoided stating the reason for the meeting, so I asked if he could give any details so Virginia and I could better prepare. He continued to be evasive."

Paul said they would clear their calendar for the following weekend, so Sandy and I made reservations and began focusing on the trip to Catalina Island, where they lived. It was to be one of the most significant trips of our life.

God's Word is true: he refuses to let sin go without consequences, but he is also faithful not to leave us without his
presence. In our case he was present through a few of our friends
at a time when we felt alone in any crowd. Although we were still
terribly confused and I was in the darkness of denial concerning
what I had done, God in his mercy and faithfulness had lifted his
banner of love over us and was surrounding us with a wall of
support and protection.

Although our attorney had advised us not to talk to anyone,
Sandy needed some support. She decided to confide in three
friends. In addition, we talked to an older couple who had been
our friends for years. These people rallied beside us and helped us
survive on a day-to-day basis. Until you have experienced the
shock of your life falling apart, it is hard to imagine the chaos and
the deep need for prayer and emotional support.

In the meantime our attorney had drafted a letter to the state
psychology board that he felt would open the door to negotiation
regarding the ethical complaint against me. It sounded good to
me. He made it seem that what I had done wasn't so bad, which
in turn strengthened my denial of the gravity of my sin and
subsequent circumstances. Now all I had to do was wait and pray
that God would help! But how little I knew of the love and
discipline of the Father. I wanted a Band-Aid; his plan included
open-heart surgery.

There were some questions that I completely ignored while in
my self-protective mode. *Does God help those who ask him to
cover up their sin and protect them from its consequences?* The
answer is obviously no—God's desire is that sin be brought to
light and then forsaken. God does not haphazardly change the
rules. *How does God help those who do not want to face themselves or their sin?* In my case, God mercifully put me in contact
with mature, caring believers whom he used to restore me to
himself.

People whose lives have caved in undergo great turmoil. Those standing in the rubble of their fallen worlds have limited awareness of their needs and no clear idea of where to begin to find help. Their immediate, emotional reactions of fear and panic often direct them away from rather than toward the help they so desperately need. The turmoil is also terrible for the innocent spouse and family.

Restoration is neither accidental nor automatic. It requires deliberate involvement. Friends around the hurting individual can best help by (1) listening kindly, (2) acknowledging the seriousness of the situation rather than assisting in the destructiveness of denial, and (3) urging the fallen person to look for help so the move toward restoration can begin.

3

Searching for an Escape— & Finding Hope

My ears were ringing as the plane left Portland and headed for Los Angeles, taking us to meet with the Friesens. Was I reacting to the noise of the engines, or just overwhelmed by the confusion within? Sandy and I didn't talk much during the flight. She had her pain, I had mine. We were together but didn't have a clue how to connect.

She asked me what I was going to say to Paul and Virginia. I said, "I don't know. I guess I'll just tell them what happened." It seemed so simple yet was so very complex. I didn't really want to tell them anything. *I've worked so hard to keep an image. Am I capable of accepting the truth about me? Am I willing to let others know who I really am?*

We made our way by shuttle from Los Angeles to Long Beach and caught the boat to Catalina Island. We had made the trip several times before as conference speakers, but I was struck by the realization that this time I was not going to the island to minister—and I was certainly not going for fun. I boarded the boat as a critically wounded person. Unlike the boat, I was without a rudder and without a compass. I was adrift, panicked, still looking for a way out.

The boat had barely cleared the jetty when I began to feel seasick. I told Sandy I needed to stay on the deck where the fresh air was blowing. I made my way to the bow of the boat where I could sit and scan the horizon for the first sight of the harbor. I struggled to keep my composure—trying not to be sick, wanting to cry, experiencing my aloneness.

I was jarred from my stupor by an announcement from the captain. There was a very large pod of dolphins just ahead. He cut the motors, and the boat drifted forward. Soon we were surrounded by marvelous diving, jumping, chattering creatures. I was filled with awe.

I felt Sandy's hand on my shoulder. As I turned to her she said, "God did this for you."

I began to cry and nodded my head in affirmation. Dolphins are my favorite animal; I have collected statues of them for years. I suddenly was surrounded by more of them than I had seen in my entire life. At that moment I realized that these dolphins were for me a symbol of the way God was surrounding me with his great love. The boat trip to Catalina was turning into a spiritual voyage far beyond what I could have imagined.

My seasickness was gone, as if carried away by the dolphins as they frolicked northward. The captain sped up the engines, and in a short time we approached the harbor. From the boat we spotted Paul and Virginia waving their arms in welcome. Virginia recalls, "We watched Earl and Sandy disembark. As they made their way up the gangplank, their body language expressed their pain and confusion. When they reached the top, we didn't talk. We just embraced and cried."

We loaded our luggage on a golf cart, the local mode of transportation, and headed up the hill to a beautiful home overlooking the harbor. Paul had arranged for us to use a friend's house, which afforded us the privacy we needed to talk plus a gorgeous view—a very sensitive gesture. We had lunch together and chatted awhile before we began to get serious. I remember staring out across the harbor, but I was hardly seeing anything. For the first time in my life I was faced with something I was incapable of making go away. I was having to face myself and my sin. I felt small and afraid.

As I told my story the fear inside me grew. I didn't want to expose myself, I didn't want to give up what I had: position, respect, authority. I wanted things to be the way they had always been.

Paul remembers:

When Earl came to see us it was clear that he wanted to know how to deal with this "unfortunate disclosure" so that his speaking ministry could continue. He wondered if it was necessary for him to take a year off. It soon became clear that he was embarrassed and possibly ashamed, but thoroughly unaware of the broad impact of his sin. A turning point in the whole process came when Virginia asked, "Is there anything else you need to confess? If you are going to clean house, you need to sweep the corners clean." Earl said that he had told us everything. He had a very long night and returned the next morning to tell us that there was actually much more that he had not shared.

I will never forget that night. I wanted my sin to remain hidden, but God wanted me to face it and give it up. As I lay in bed beside my emotionally exhausted wife, I was confronted by the most important questions I have ever faced. *Are you willing to confess all? Are you willing to repent? Are you willing to expose all of your sin and to give it up?*

I tried to convince God that the details didn't have to come out—I would deal with it on my own. I told him I didn't want Sandy to be hurt even further. *And what about the kids, Lord?* But God remained firm. In my mind I began to see it as a life-or-death choice. I remembered the many Scriptures where the admonition to choose life is presented. *But it isn't life, Lord. It will kill me.* I was still refusing to repent. I wanted my way and not God's way.

The battle continued until about 4 a.m. Then I gave in. I remember saying, *Okay, God, I'll tell everything. I want life. I want you. I want my wife and my family.* These were faith affirmations. My human nature could not imagine that confessing all my sins could possibly lead to life—it seemed instead that life would be stripped away from me. I had to make an about-face; I had to trust God. I couldn't solve this myself. I had to see my life and my sin as God sees them, not as I had seen them. Could I expose myself to the point that I could give up the old lifestyle?

Yes, I will! I finally concluded. And then, interestingly enough, I slept the rest of the night. This was the turning point in the process toward restoration. Without coming to that point of repentance, there would be no restoration. The entire house had to be cleaned, every corner.

When the four of us got together the next morning, I confessed that I had lied to Virginia the previous evening and that I was involved in more sin than I had first admitted. I could not share many details right then, but I agreed to write down everything and share it with Sandy, Paul and Virginia the next time we met. (The whole truth was that I was giving in regularly to a sexual addiction—not only the affair but also the use of pornography and visits to massage parlors, prostitutes and nude bars.)

Sandy was filled with fear and questions. She remembers thinking, *What more will I hear?* "I felt a flood of many emotions. Fear gripped me about what he would write in the letter. Would it be too much for me to handle? On the other hand, I was cautiously hopeful that he would be willing to sweep the corners clean through a full confession. I knew that would be the only hope we'd have to rebuild."

My search for an escape was changing to a search for help and hope. I was beginning to get in touch with reality and to take some responsibility for moving toward wholeness. I asked Paul to supervise my spiritual recovery, and he agreed. By my request I was giving him a lot of authority in my life. I knew that our lives would be intimately linked. We spent the last hours together dealing with some of the specifics of this new relationship. Paul and Virginia asked us to find another couple in the Portland area who would also become a part of the process. Thus the idea of the Spiritual Care Team was born.

Now came the difficult realities. Paul asked me to withdraw from all speaking and writing, to curtail counseling ministry and to consider myself as a new Christian. He said, "You know a lot about God, but you have not been living in accordance with what you know."

These words were hard for me to hear, but in my heart I knew they were true. The memory is vivid for Paul.

Although there were many tears shed during our weekend together, nothing compared to what we experienced in the last hours. We had talked about who to tell, what to tell, how to tell. The one remaining question was what to do about future ministry opportunities. I had asked Earl all weekend what he thought would be most appropriate. He had remained silent. He still couldn't verbalize what actions should be taken.

Finally I told him I felt he should cancel all speaking engagements, suspend writing projects, resign from his seminary teaching position, and terminate all positions of leadership for a minimum of two years. He would be left with only his work as a psychologist, and that was also in jeopardy. We had heard a lot of crying during the weekend, but nothing could compare with the gut-wrenching wailing that this pronouncement evoked. It was as if I had grabbed the insides of Earl, his very essence, and had ripped it from him. His significance and worth seemed so totally tied to his writing, speaking and teaching.

Sandy recalls, "I was angry that Earl's most desperate wailing was uttered over his not being allowed to take speaking engagements. What about *me?* He had cried much less over the possibility of losing me. It was so perplexing. I felt devalued and overwhelmed."

Before we left the island we agreed that we would get together in Portland during the first week of December. I told Paul I would have my full confession written by the time of our meeting. We would try to find another couple to serve on the Spiritual Care Team. We also talked about how to let our children know. I knew that their lives would be devastated, and I dreaded their reaction. I was now facing enough reality to understand that I would be a source of pain for them, but I was still too self-centered to realize how deeply crushed they would be. Paul and Virginia committed to pray for us and sent us on our way.

Paul describes his feelings following our departure:

After our weekend with Earl and Sandy, we realized we were being asked to help them navigate uncharted waters with unknown reefs and shoals. Our decision to participate in the voyage had to be made without knowledge of all the risks. We felt ill-equipped for the journey. Had it not been for the assurance that God was at the helm, we never would have boarded the ship.

I was exhausted as the boat bounced across the waves for the twenty-six miles back to Long Beach. I was more devastated than I could have ever imagined, and yet growing within me was a small glimmer of optimism: maybe there was hope. The wailing inside began to dissipate. *What's next, Lord?* I wondered. I was used to mapping out every step of my life, and now I couldn't even imagine any next steps.

In the beginning Sandy had raised the question of my going to a therapist, but I had initially brushed it off. Where does a therapist find a therapist? Later I agreed to go if I could find the "right person." My arrogance said, "I don't need help from anyone. I can help myself." Sandy's concern and prayer was that God would lead me to someone who was tough enough to make me look at myself and deal with the real issues in my life.

Although I didn't pray a lot about it, God was at work, and he brought to my mind the name of Daniel McIvor. I had attended workshops that Dr. McIvor had conducted for the Washington State Psychological Association. I liked and respected him; more important, I remembered his talking about the problem of lying by omission. I was beginning to realize that my problems were not just sexual but revolved around a lifestyle of lying and deceit. Up until this time, had I been asked if I was a liar, I would have been offended and would have answered with an emphatic "No!" Sadly, I would have believed I was telling the truth.

Although Dr. McIvor's practice was located 225 miles from Portland, I called and made an appointment for mid-November. I told Sandy I thought he could help me get a handle on things rather quickly. I thought one or two sessions would resolve my issues. I laugh now at the extent to which I was minimizing the problem.

Although I could not see it at the time, God was putting together for me and for Sandy the resources he wanted to use to restore me to himself and to give us new life. It was clear that the loving Father was not abandoning us or letting me go. He would not let me escape. For the first time, I had hope that change might be possible.

4

The Formation of the Spiritual Care Team

*B**y the time we returned* home from Catalina, two significant things had occurred. I had begun the process of repentance by taking the first step of confession. And God had given us a couple to lead us in the recovery process. Still, significant as that was, it felt like so little when our need was so great.

Sandy and I had talked about who else might come alongside us in the restoration process. After considering many couples, we felt God directing us to Larry and Nancy Paulson. We didn't know them very well, but we had belonged to the same church at one time, and they seemed like caring and spiritually balanced people.

We decided that I should contact Larry, tell him the story and request their participation. I was really frightened. I knew Larry respected me; I feared that my confession would obliterate this respect forever. I struggled with not wanting to tell him what I had done, then wrestled with a desire to gloss over things and make the picture much brighter than it was. I was beginning to understand that the truth needed to be told in all its bleakness if my healing was to continue. We met for lunch, and among the tears and salad dressing I asked if he and Nancy would join the team.

Larry reflects on that meeting: "When Earl first asked Nancy and me to participate in the process, my initial reaction was fear—in two respects. My first fear was personal: I knew this would involve soul-searching, in terms not only of my own sins but also of my relationship with my wife. The second fear dealt with inadequacy: I would be attempting to help a person who had a Ph.D. in psychology and was married to a counselor with a master's degree."

Larry said he would talk with Nancy and let me know in a couple of days. I felt relieved, comforted and fearful all at once. My heart was lighter as I drove home. At least one more step had been taken.

Nancy recalls in detail her conversation with Larry. Her recollections reveal some of the struggles that a prospective care team member may face.

"I need to talk to you, and I think you'd better sit down," Larry announced as he walked through the back door after his lunch with Earl. He went on to divulge the pathetic truth about Earl's life and his request for our support.

I had admired this man. Now revulsion, confusion and anger zigzagged through me. I didn't want to hear this. At that moment I perceived Earl as phony, deceptive and sick. I had no desire to get involved. I was very disillusioned. *Where are you, God? These kinds of failures seem to destroy your credibility.*

Pondering the idea of counseling two professional counselors defused my self-confidence. Inadequacy loomed up like a flashing red light, stopping me from believing God was nudging me to accept this call. No question—I was out of my spiritual league! Was I willing to risk crawling out on faith's ledge and say I would help? I have a tendency to accept only those tasks I know I can do well. This is where Christianity gets uncomfortable. I found myself arguing with God and losing.

But what about Sandy and the children? I wondered. Just considering their devastation diluted my argument. Compassion and concern for them drew me closer to the prospect of accepting the call. God persisted, and I decided he was calling me to be available.

I felt uncomfortable as I anticipated the first meeting of the Spiritual Care Team. I had never met the Friesens, and I knew Earl was going to expose his life to all of us. Our initial greeting was awkward. I struggled with what to say. My discomfort dissipated when Paul Friesen opened our meeting with prayer. Then, trembling and in tears, Earl revealed his situation in such detail that I wanted to plug my ears and close my eyes in hopes of escaping.

Grow up, Nancy, and face the real world! I told myself. I watched Sandy as she patted Earl's knee and reached out to hold his sweaty, shaky hand. Tears filled her eyes. I was amazed at her compassion. It became contagious. Here was a broken man destroyed by sin but begging for help. How could I refuse? I felt I was there because Earl needed my husband's stability and I came with the package. I wasn't sure what my role would be, but I wanted to help.

Our Biblical Mandate

The Spiritual Care Team was complete. Besides adopting a biblical mandate, the members agreed on some logistical and procedural commitments early in the process. They committed themselves to the following steps:

1. To be in regular communication with both Sandy and me.
2. To pray regularly for us.

3. To meet as a team quarterly until the process was complete. (Ideally the team should meet more often; due to geographical distance, quarterly was all our team could manage.)

4. To consult with others who had experience in restoration ministry.

5. To hold me accountable to my promises (did I confess to _____? did I send my letter of resignation to the seminary?).

Though none of us had a master plan or even a well-formulated view of what restoration entailed, the team was committed to looking to the Spirit of God to lead us, to gleaning truth from Scripture and to seeking wise counsel.

Our biblical mandate came from Galatians 6:1; it gave clear direction to the team. Paul reflects on what we discovered from this passage.

Galatians 6:1 reads, "Brothers, if someone is caught in a sin, you who are spiritual should restore him gently. But watch yourself, or you also may be tempted." The passage seems to be saying that one of the "costs" of caring for those who are fallen is an increased susceptibility to temptation yourself. A good friend of mine expressed concern for my own purity during this process. At first I thought his concern to be quite unusual and unfounded. Because temptations have confronted me since then, I have come to realize the wisdom of his statement.The assumption that my involvement with one entangled in sexual sin would sicken me to the point of revulsion to any such temptation was unfounded. My thought that exposure to the far-reaching, gut-wrenching ramifications of such evil would immunize me from any temptation was wrong also. Such faulty logic leads to complacency or even arrogance in regards to the possibility of moral failure.

The Galatians 6 passage also speaks of a process. It doesn't say restore him quickly. It says restore him "gently." Gentle restoration takes time. Two meanings of the word *restore* in this passage are to set bones straight so they can mend and to repair a tear, such as in a fishing net. These definitions clearly speak of a process that takes time. The idea of instant restoration is not within the scope of the meaning of this word.

And so we agreed that Galatians 6:1 would be the theme verse of the restoration process. It spoke of time involvement and inherent risks, and it gave us instructions for working with Earl and for safeguarding ourselves. Though many unresolved issues still faced us, this verse provided clear direction and hope.

One of the issues was developing a clear-cut definition of a Spiritual Care Team. This issue was pressed by Daniel McIvor, my therapist, in a conversation he had with Paul Friesen. After I signed a release, Paul called Dr. McIvor.

"So, what are you?" asked Dr. McIvor. "Are you Earl's counselors, therapists or what?"

I thought a second before replying, "Well, we are people who care about Earl and Sandy and who want to encourage them and hold Earl accountable in this process of restoration."

By his question, it was clear that Dr. McIvor had not experienced the concept of a Spiritual Care Team before and was not quite sure what to think of it.

After trying to sound convincing about what we were, I did have to ask myself the question *Why are we doing this?* Earl had a therapist; wasn't that enough? We weren't even trained counselors. What did we have to offer? Yet from the vantage point of seven years of hindsight, I now have a much clearer and more complete response to Dr. McIvor's question.

The short answer Paul gave that day in December 1989 is still valid, but the following thoughts expand on the function of the Spiritual Care Team and how they encouraged us and held me accountable.

We have identified the following six purposes of a Spiritual Care Team:

1. Spiritual health. The Spiritual Care Team is appropriately named. It is a team of people committed to providing care for a wounded member of the body of Christ. A counselor or therapist may work in specific areas of pathology, but the Spiritual Care Team is interested in ferreting out the spiritual roots of the problem. The Spiritual Care Team is also interested in helping the individual come to a place of spiritual health. The team focuses not only on the specific sin, but on the whole area of spiritual growth. A therapist may help the person to change certain behavior patterns, but the emphasis of the Spiritual Care Team is to help the person become grounded anew in a relationship with the living God.

2. Body life. The Spiritual Care Team brings together different spiritual gifts that, when combined, can unleash God's love and power to the restoree. Gifts such as intercession, discernment, admonishment, encouragement, mercy and serving are part of the job description for a team member.

3. Accountability and sensitivity. The Spiritual Care Team acts as an advocate for the spouse or family members who have also been injured. Often the sinner has fooled the spouse and made him or her feel responsible for the sinner's actions. Including the spouse and other family members (as appropriate) in the Spiritual Care Team allows the team to hear and stand by them, freeing them to speak truthfully and ask questions. The Spiritual Care Team holds the sinner accountable to correct harmful patterns toward family members and others in order to rebuild relationships with them.

4. Penetrating denial and clarifying reality. Often the one who has fallen into sin is a powerful person who is able to intimidate those around him or her and convincingly present a distorted view of reality, seeking to impose it on others. The advantage of having multiple members on the team is that it is more difficult to distort the facts or intimidate a whole group. Sandy remembers, "Knowing my insecurities, Earl could easily have out-talked me had I not been supported by others. More than once I was able to stand up to Earl because I knew four others would stand with me." A spouse or family member who might otherwise be too wounded, confused or insecure to stand alone will benefit from the strength and support of the team.

5. Synergy. A Spiritual Care Team benefits from the wisdom found in the company of others. It is an awesome responsibility to have someone voluntarily put himself or herself under your care for a period of time, so the combined wisdom and consensus of the group, led by the Spirit of God, is very important.

6. Intercession. The Spiritual Care Team is committed to interceding on behalf of the restoree, the family and those who fall within the sphere of the person's influence. Praying for God's mercy, strength and restoration is probably the most critical function of the team. Restoration ministry is divine in nature and is characterized above all by grace. It cannot be driven by anything apart from consistent intercession.

Criteria for Selection

Our team was formed within two months of my initial confession to Sandy. The primary consideration of the other two couples was to surround Sandy and me with the best help they could provide. The selection of our team was the result of intuitive processing and divine guidance. Now, seven years later, we have distilled some criteria for selection of a strong team.

Acts 6:1-6 provides the foundational criteria that we believe cannot be compromised. This passage records the account of the selection of deacons in the early church. Two standards for selection are presented: "full of the Spirit and wisdom" implies that a deacon (1) should be characterized by a vital, authentic, growing relationship with the Lord and (2) should have gained wisdom as an outgrowth of that relationship. These standards should be employed in selecting Spiritual Care Team members as well.

In addition to having the above spiritual qualifications, Spiritual Care Team members should be people who, though imperfect, are

☐ emotionally and spiritually mature

☐ compassionate care-givers

☐ committed to keeping confidences

☐ humble

☐ trustworthy

☐ cooperative

☐ not easily intimidated; willing to confront hard issues

☐ strongly committed to truth

☐ willing to engage in self-examination

☐ willing to commit time

☐ willing to commit finances if necessary

☐ willing to enter into the process of suffering

☐ willing to endure guilt by association if necessary

☐ willing to face personal and family issues of their own that may arise as the result of team involvement—in particular, husband-wife conflicts and loss of family time

Besides these characteristics, there are also a number of practical issues that need to be considered when forming a Spiritual Care Team.

1. Involvement in patterns of sin severely changes the family system. Team members need to be involved in restructuring the family's patterns. The spouse and the family of the restoree need support and guidance through this process. Sometimes it may be as simple a thing as suggesting new ways of spending time together or insisting that family interaction be given a higher priority.

2. Long-term practice of sin often relies on habits of secrecy and cover-up that must be rooted out and destroyed if the sinner

is to be restored. Team members must ask hard questions and relentlessly push for the truth.

3. The restoration process can be best coordinated through the local church. Preexisting relationships found there can provide sources for both accountability and support. The local church also has the opportunity to learn from and be strengthened by the ongoing restoration process.

We do not, however, recommend that the pastor be on the Spiritual Care Team. There are at least three practical reasons for this position:

☐ The time commitment is immense, and few pastors' schedules can absorb that much additional output.

☐ The potential exists for more than one Spiritual Care Team functioning at one time within a church.

☐ The family in crisis needs the pastor to fulfill his pastoral role with them, and that may be compromised if the pastor is part of the team.

The pastor should be involved in the process by being informed of progress and by supporting and praying for the efforts of the team. (In a large church with a multiple pastoral staff, a pastor from that staff could be a team member.)

4. The restoree and his or her spouse, where applicable, should have a voice in the selection of Spiritual Care Team members. Although the restoree is not in the best position to understand his or her own needs, a minimal comfort level with Spiritual Care Team members is essential. Restoration requires submission to the authority of the team, so it is important that the team is made up of people the restoree respects.

5. A possible side effect of involvement in a Spiritual Care Team can be a loss of innocence on the part of team members. The confession of sin may become more graphic than team members would ever care to see or hear. But remember: bringing sin to the light is critical to the restoration process.

6. Be careful to select team members who will pray faithfully throughout the extended restoration process. This unique ministry requires a great deal from the team. The importance of prayer cannot be overstated.

7. A good number for a Spiritual Care Team is four to six people in addition to the person being restored and, if married, his or her spouse. Preferably, the team should be comprised of both men and women.

The concept of Spiritual Care Teams can empower churches to come alongside their wounded members in effective, life-giving service and can help break the pattern of "shooting our wounded." Spiritual Care Teams flesh out the ministry of Jesus very tangibly to those whose only hope is in him. Our prayer is that this model will equip the body of Christ with the tools necessary to "restore [them] gently" (Gal 6:1).

5

What Is Restoration?

In January 1994 a major earthquake hit Southern California. Freeways buckled, public utilities were severely damaged, homes were destroyed and lives were lost. Chaos and confusion reigned. What would it take to repair the damage and restore the community to some sense of order?

It is not enough just to repair buildings and roads; they must be made stronger than they were before the quake. Engineers call this "retrofitting"—bringing physical structures to a place of greater strength and stability *after* they've been built. Retrofitting bridges, buildings and freeways is necessary due to the possibility of future natural disasters. A building weakened by one earthquake could easily crumble with the next quake unless improvements are made. The goal is to be prepared so that future shocks will not result in total destruction.

When a Personal Earthquake Hits
This concept presents a visual image of what happens inside a

person whose choices cause the devastation of a major life earthquake. It also pictures the extensive efforts needed to rebuild that life. Hebrews 12:12-13 tells us, "Strengthen your feeble arms and weak knees. Make level paths for your feet, so that the lame may not be disabled, but rather healed." This passage teaches the principle of *spiritual reconstruction*, which leads to healing.

The earthquake analogy teaches us an important lesson about weaknesses in a structure that are not visible prior to the quake. Post-earthquake inspection of a crumbled structure may reveal internal weaknesses that contributed to its collapse. The same is true in personal disasters. An effective restoration process must deal not only with the ruin of the disaster, but also with the internal, preexisting weaknesses that caused it. Sinful choices, such as adultery or living a double life, are not made in a vacuum. They are made because the person involved in sin has not built enough integrity into his or her internal structure. Anyone who ignores the need to live by biblical truths is vulnerable.

Hebrews 10:19-25 reminds us that the foundation of our faith is Jesus Christ. The strength of our internal structure and integrity comes through our holding "unswervingly to the hope we profess." Our periodic inspections take place when we "[meet] together" to "consider how we may spur one another on toward love and good deeds." Just as it is arrogant to declare that we have built a structure that is able to withstand any earthquake, so it is arrogant to declare that we have equipped ourselves well and will never fall. In both structures and lives, however, careful building and maintenance can greatly reduce the likelihood of a serious disaster.

This principle is illustrated by the life of Bill, a pastor in need of restoration. Bill had attended Bible college and seminary with only one purpose in mind: to equip himself to serve the Lord he loved. He never intended to become an alcoholic or a gambling addict.

His gifts were polished over a period of years, and he was recognized as a man who bore the mark and the blessing of God. Yet the gambling came to light when his wife discovered large, unexplained cash withdrawals on their charge cards. During the same span of years he began to violate his own stated beliefs regarding the use of alcohol. Drinking became an acceptable way of dulling the pain caused by his dual lifestyle and the physical problems that had developed.

What happened? What are the steps that led to his tearful resignation from his church? What is the weakness in his internal structure that brought him to such a place? If restoration for Bill is to happen, these are the questions the Spiritual Care Team must address.

Bill's self-destructive slide began when he became curious about gambling and tried it out. He was saying *I might get lucky* when he should have been saying *I need to stay away from this.* As always happens, when he refused to flee he got in over his head. Soon he was in debt. His next self-destructive step was to keep it a secret from his wife. He also got deeper into self-deceit by telling himself, *I'll win back the money, and no one will know.*

The cycle went from greater debt to more emotional pain to heavier drinking. His pattern of internal weakness and bad choices took its toll. By the time Bill met with his Spiritual Care Team he was a defeated man teetering on the brink of destruction.

So where does the team begin? The external damage is obvious: addiction to drugs and alcohol, large gambling debts, physical health problems.

Sobriety and major lifestyle adjustments can be readily identified by team members as desirable goals, and these often become the focal point of restoration. They are not, however, what restoration is all about. If they are all that is addressed, the real work will not get done. The team and the individual must pinpoint external damage and internal weaknesses and begin the retrofitting process. If those involved in the ministry of restoration accept this challenge, the restoree will be not only healed but also strengthened.

In Bill's case, there was a willingness to face who he had become. He wondered at times if he could go on, but he did. He faced each weakness as the team brought it to his attention, and God honored his desire for restoration.

People who live in earthquake-prone areas are always on guard. They know where to stand if the building they are in begins to shake. In the same way, temptations will inevitably confront us, even in areas in which we feel impenetrable, and will often strike when we least expect them. As Gordon MacDonald quotes, "An unguarded strength becomes a double weakness" (*Rebuilding Your Broken World* [Nashville: Nelson, 1988], p. 47). Perhaps that is what Solomon had in mind when he wrote, "The highway of the upright avoids evil; he who guards his way guards his life. Pride goes before destruction, a haughty spirit before a fall" (Prov 16:17-18).

Retrofitting is an important and wonderful process that saves many buildings in the long run, but remember that the better way is to build the structure with strength, flexibility and integrity the first time around. This is true in our lives as well. If our internal structure is built on biblical principles, when crises hit we will experience less down time and lower reconstruction costs—and there will be fewer injuries to others.

Strengthening the Foundation

The foundation for restoration is reconciliation with God. It begins with God's working in the heart of the one whose choices have led him or her into sin and separation from God. God wants to be in relationship with his children. The restoree loses sight of this truth and often believes that God has no use for him or her. For someone to desire restoration, he or she needs a renewed view of God's mercy and his demand for personal holiness.

Malachi 3:7 tells us, " 'Return to me, and I will return to you,' says the LORD Almighty." The word *return* is very important in this book. The ministry of restoration involves encouraging a fallen saint to return to fellowship with God and with God's family. Returning is possible because the blood of Jesus Christ cleanses us from all sins (1 Jn 1:9) and because God extends his mercy to us so that we can return to him.

My own personal earthquake devastated me. Being exposed was not an unjust thing; it was what needed to happen. But along with justice I needed mercy. God's mercy toward me became real through the words of Lamentations 3:22-23: "Because of the LORD's great love we are not consumed, for his compassions never fail." These words were a constant source of comfort and encouragement to me throughout my restoration process. I was beginning to understand God's call for my personal holiness through the words of 1 Peter 1:16: "Be holy, because I am holy." The truth of these verses was moving me toward reconciliation with God. I was being retrofitted from the inside out.

Choosing to Rebuild

When a person falls into sin, one of three things will happen.

1. The person will choose not to repent.

2. The person will feign repentance and receive a pseudo-restoration.

3. The person will repent and be restored.

What actually happens depends on the choice of the sinner. The Spiritual Care Team can encourage, direct and exhort, but the sinner must choose whether he or she *really* wants to pursue restoration.

1. Choosing not to repent. Our hearts are saddened when we learn that a person we have loved and admired has chosen to follow sinful desires rather than to follow the Savior. It is even sadder when we learn that a person has been confronted with personal sin and has chosen not to turn from the chosen path to destruction. Jesus felt such sorrow; he looked at the city of Jerusalem and wept over its unrepentance: "O Jerusalem, Jerusalem, you who kill the prophets and stone those sent to you, how often I have longed to gather your children together, as a hen gathers her chicks under her wings, but you were not willing" (Mt 23:37).

The key words in the verse are *not willing*. The restoration process does not fail because God is reluctant or unable; it fails because the potential restoree is unwilling. Those who care about the person can offer love and accountability, but the choice is up to the individual.

One of the members of our Spiritual Care Team was asked to consult with a church who wished to confront their pastor regarding what they saw as a potentially dangerous situation with a woman staff member. During the meeting with the church board, the consultant asked the board, "If your pastor is willing to receive your admonishment to holiness and to end this dangerous relationship in order to fulfill the requirement of Scripture for leadership to be blameless [in Greek, "unaccused" or "irreproachable"; see 1 Tim 3:10], will you be willing to continue to follow his leadership?" Each person in the room responded without hesitation, "Yes!" There seemed to be an excitement that a healthy resolution could occur. The board made plans to talk to the pastor, and the consultant returned home, tired but satisfied.

Three days later he received a sad telephone call. "We met with the pastor, but he was unwilling to follow our suggestion. He resigned on the spot and is packing to leave town." Later it was learned that the pastor had left his family and did not pursue either personal restoration or further ministry. He was *unwilling*—unwilling to return to a life of holiness, to his family, to fellowship with his church family or to his vocation. What a sad loss for all involved.

2. *Pseudo-restoration.* A false repentance may seem desirable—the person caught in sin just wants to get the whole thing over with as quickly as possible. We are uncomfortable and don't know what to do, so we adopt an "out of sight, out of mind" policy or subscribe to the "let's just put this behind us" philosophy. These attitudes do little to promote restoration and instead create an atmosphere in which the exterior damage is covered over while the interior structural damage is ignored and unhealed.

When Jim was caught embezzling money from his company, he lost his job, and word filtered through the church. The rumor mill suggested that he was sorry and that his employer hadn't really treated him very fairly. (We are often quick to help people justify their sin. This is not a part of the restoration process.) Jim did not approach the elders or the pastor with his predicament. Repentance was assumed; no one cared enough to really check it out. After the initial shock waves subsided, people in the church didn't pay much attention to Jim. In fact, no one had much interaction with him. If asked, church members were quick to say they had heard he was doing okay. They were willing to assume that Jim was okay now, or that if he wasn't it was none of their business. His burdens were not being borne by anyone, and his personal growth and development were ignored. It was assumed that he was restored primarily because he did return to church and had found a new job. No one really knew about his current spiritual condition.

In pseudo-restoration the family is seldom helped. No one asks the children about their needs. No one helps them address their shame and disillusionment. The spouse often stands alone during those long hours, trying to decide whether or not the sinning partner can ever be trusted.

We often overlook the fact that sinful choices have a devastating impact not only on the life of the individual making them, but also on the lives of family members, friends and colleagues. Gordon MacDonald rightly refers to both the one committing the sin and those affected by it as "broken-world people." He asks, "And what of those who live with the side effects of broken-world choices? the betrayed spouse? the cheated business partner? the exploited friend? the deceived employer? They often live with a pain they can hardly describe, and they ask hard questions about their rights and their responsibilities. In the final analysis, few broken-world people touch only one life. Like a hand grenade, the effects of one person's terrible choices explode outward to wound many others" (*Rebuilding Your Broken World* [Nashville: Nelson, 1988], p. 35).

In Jim's situation, it would be premature to evaluate and label his restoration complete, pseudo- or nonexistent, but many danger signs exist. His story highlights a tremendous lack of burden-bearing. No one stood in the gap; no one asked the hard questions; no one was willing to hold Jim accountable; no one became concerned about relapse. Confession does not assure either repentance or rejection of sin. When a person says he is sorry, he has not told you a whole lot. He may simply mean he is sorry that he was caught. He may be embarrassed but not repentant. Integral to the ministry of restoration is a clear understanding of whether or not the person has changed direction and a commitment to help him install barriers that will prevent him from turning back. No one is asking Jim the hard questions that could bring about the cleansing and change he needs.

When the sinning individual wants to continue life as before and does not want to deal with the consequences of sinful choices, often the person is only interested in pseudo-restoration or a quick cover-up. Churches often promote this problem by saying, "Aren't we supposed to just forgive and forget?" As a restoree, I register an emphatic "No!" I need to thoroughly deal with my sin and the devastating consequences of it in order to complete the repentance process.

You might ask, "Why? Why can't we just forgive and forget? Why can't we just move on?" The answer is that I, as a sinner, have spent hours, days, possibly years denying the truth that my sin has consequences for me, for those I have sinned against and for innocent bystanders. I do not need to be continually confronted with what I've done, but neither should I be allowed to deny the impact my sin has had on me and others or to slip back into familiar sinful ways. God lets me, and all of us, remember our sins and the consequences so that we will not return to them. Complete restoration is impeded when we don't help wayward Christians examine the full extent of the shambles their sin has caused.

In John 21 Jesus conducts his ministry of restoration for Peter. Peter had boasted at the time of the Last Supper that he was willing to be imprisoned or even die because his love for Jesus Christ was so strong (see Luke 22:31-34). A careful study of John 21:15-19 reveals that Jesus takes Peter back to that vain proclamation by questioning three times Peter's love for him. Is he rubbing Peter's nose in it? Is this a method of punishment chosen by Jesus to further humiliate or shame Peter? No; I think Jesus is simply calling attention to the problem so that Peter will not lose sight of the defectiveness of his internal structure. Peter's sin was not just denial of Jesus. It also involved arrogance and pride, which had to be dealt with before restoration could occur. Jesus was thorough so that the restoration Peter experienced would be complete.

3. True restoration. The positive impact of restoration begins when the one being restored has confessed all sin and is no longer living in secrecy and denial. These choices and actions clear the path for involvement in the restoration process. I cannot overemphasize the importance of restoration being seen as a process rather than an event surrounding confession. The restoration process requires renewed involvement with God, the family and other believers who are connected to the person. And it involves commitment to the restoration team.

During the process of true restoration the heart of the person being restored is open to God's discipline, grace and mercy and to direction from the Spiritual Care Team. A repentant person is freed from defensiveness. As my own restoration process progressed, I found myself more and more open to suggestions. I saw the Spiritual Care Team as my allies rather than my enemies. I wanted input from them because I realized that I had blind spots that could not be corrected unless I allowed the team, my wife and my therapist to point them out to me. This was a conscious decision. Following repentance, it was the most important decision I made during the restoration process. This has changed my view of the role God intends us to play in each others' lives. We need each other more than I ever realized.

Conclusion

Choices to go against God; choices to serve the self and violate long-standing principles; choices to disregard the impact of one's behavior on relationships with God, family and friends—these eventually lead to a shattered life. The ministry of restoration must address that life and the process that led to its destruction. Restoration can begin only when the person who made so many wrong choices comes to the place of facing those choices—and chooses to turn from them.

Gordon MacDonald writes, "There are no words to describe the inner anguish of knowing that you have disappointed and offended God, that you have violated your own integrity, and that you have betrayed people you really love and care for" (*Rebuilding Your Broken World,* p. 163). Restoration cannot occur until the sinning individual views his or her life from this perspective. One of the tasks of the Spiritual Care Team is to keep this idea clearly in mind so that the restoree will not abandon the process.

It is critical that the Spiritual Care Team not only help in the process of full repentance but also constantly encourage the fallen one with the promise of new life that awaits him or her at the end of the process. Psalm 32:1-5 states that the lack of acknowledgment of our sin results in our "wasting away." As the fallen sinner confesses, there is blessing, and the Lord does not count that sin against one "in whose spirit is no deceit" (v. 2).

Repentance is hard and painful work. But it does result in freedom from enslavement to sin and in a relationship with the Father that is possible only after the forgiveness of sin. After confessing to her husband that she had been unfaithful, one woman wrote,

These have been extremely difficult times, but we now are building on a bedrock of honesty. I have never before experienced the true intimacy that my husband and I now have. Now we are "naked and unashamed" before each other, and it feels so good.

Continue to press on with the process of repentance; resist the urge to short-circuit the process, for at the end is the hope of a brighter day.

6

Going Against the Grain

S*hortly after Sandy* and I returned from Catalina, we began to face some major dilemmas regarding restoration issues. After I had composed the letter to Sandy describing the extent of my sin, I was advised by a pastor friend not to share the letter with her. He felt it would be too painful for Sandy to receive such full disclosure.

I gave the letter to her anyway. Sandy remembers, "Even though the letter was devastating, I felt relief. Perhaps now we could move ahead, because the whole gory mess was finally on the table."

As we related my situation to close friends and colleagues, people were quick to say "I forgive you" and provide explanations or excuses for what I had done. They were attempting to avoid pain and to shelter me from responsibility. Such rationalizations presented on my behalf tempted me to deny what I had done and to take an easy way out. At times Sandy and I became confused and felt like the battle for recovery and restoration was not just an uphill battle, but a battle waged against the grain of popular Christian practice.

During the course of the formal restoration process, several "against the grain" issues arose. Sandy and I, with the Spiritual Care Team, had to carefully and prayerfully work through each one. Every time Sandy or I met with Dr. McIvor, he would ask questions that would cause me, and Sandy to a lesser degree, to face issues of disclosure and accountability. It was painful at times, but I wanted to get well, so I had to go against the grain. I couldn't avoid pain. I had to grow. Secrecy kills; only truth heals.

It is possible to lose or deny important truths and principles of restoration if you do not realize that popular Christian thought may encourage distortion or pulling back from truth. Some major issues of distortion are presented in this chapter so that you can understand them and choose the way of truth.

Against-the-Grain Issues

Disclosure versus secrecy. To tell or not to tell; to hide or not to hide; to confess or not to confess—"what people don't know won't hurt them" seems to be the popular view and the practice in most churches. "Keep it under wraps; there's no reason to hurt others or to get people upset."

But our against-the-grain view is that secrecy, which is a form of darkness, encourages sin. Only disclosure brings sin to the light where it can be fully dealt with by the sinner, the victims, the innocent parties and those who live in a world filled with temptation.

Recently Paul Friesen preached a sermon entitled "Honesty and Intimacy." In it he shared the story of my sin and the restoration process. The congregation was shocked when Paul said, "The man's name is Earl Wilson. I am telling you Earl's story with his permission and for his good. You see, it was secrecy that allowed him to continue in sin as deeply and as long as he did."

We say that we desire intimacy in our churches, yet we practice secrecy. We change people's names when we're relating a story in order to protect the innocent, when in fact we're protecting the guilty. It is only when we help the guilty to see their guilt, accept responsibility, repent, and receive forgiveness and restoration that we are truly protecting them. Protection happens most naturally when full disclosure takes place.

Accountability versus tolerance. The 1990s has been called the decade of tolerance. Anything goes; what other people do is none of my business. We hide behind the phrase "That's between her and God." We may think, *I don't agree with what she's doing,* but our silence seems to shout, "It is none of my business; I don't want to get involved!"

The model of restoration presented here takes the view that we are our brother's keeper; we *must* get involved. Accountability— the most loving thing to do—calls sin *sin* and stands firmly against it. Tolerance, the politically correct approach, is the popular view, but it does not lead to restoration. Being politically correct implies that we will never say things that might cause us to lose favor with others. We attempt to talk without being offensive. In a tolerant Christian society, being politically correct takes precedence over being intellectually correct, scientifically correct, religiously correct, even biblically correct. This view is incompatible with restoration.

The Spiritual Care Team's against-the-grain position is that restoration cannot occur unless tolerance and political correctness are replaced by a call to accountability—a call made by people who are willing to be involved in the healing process. If restoration is to occur, those working toward it must not be confused by thinking that tolerance of sin or avoidance of talking about sin will help to restore the sinner gently. Such an approach doesn't restore at all—it prevents restoration.

Community versus individuality. Talk of Christian community is popular, but real community is not often practiced in any depth within our churches. We live in the era of personal isolation: *I can do it myself. I can restore myself. I can return to God all by myself. I can stop sinning all by myself. I don't need anyone else.* If someone says, "I have taken care of things," we do not question the process.

The instruction of Galatians 6:1-2, the guiding theme of my Spiritual Care Team, is the opposite of this type of thinking: "If someone is caught in a sin, you who are spiritual should restore him gently. But watch yourself, or you also may be tempted. Carry each other's burdens, and in this way you will fulfill the law of Christ." These verses call Christians and the entire Christian community to loving, active involvement in each other's lives.

Unfortunately, all too often Christians ignore the Scriptures related to community and pause only briefly to consider the wisdom of such sayings as the oft-quoted African proverb "It takes a village to raise a child." How large a village does it take to restore a fallen sinner? We aren't sure. But one thing we know is that restoration rarely if ever happens when left to the individual sinner. Restoration involves relationships that help the restoree relate to God and others again in positive and appropriate ways.

Recently a man who is involved as a member of a restoration team, in recalling his own past moral failure, lamented, "If only there had been something like this for me when I committed my great sin! I wasted years and years stumbling around trying to find my way back to God on my own." In a Christian community, one person's sin affects everyone. So everyone should bear the responsibility of being part of the restoration.

Winebrenner and Frazier give enthusiastic support for this approach:

What a privilege to be a vessel of grace and restoration. To open our homes, to give honest guidance, to shield one from hurt, to give of our time and money and emotions, to laugh and weep. When he's hard on himself, we are God's gentle reminder of forgiveness. When she feels unloved, we are God's affirmation of love. When he's being left out, we walk alongside. When we hear rumors and gossip, we speak the truth in love.

"We can welcome examination by the world if we acknowledge sin, confront honest anger and hurt and confusion, and end with a collective commitment to restore the fallen and a determination to not frustrate God's grace" (Jan Winebrenner and Debra Frazier, *When a Leader Falls, What Happens to Everyone Else?* [Minneapolis: Bethany House, 1993], p. 68).

Shifting blame versus admitting guilt. There is a game played in many churches these days where we say to each other, thinking this is the loving thing to do, "If you confess your sin or weakness, I will help you minimize or deny it. If you tell me your sin, I will tell you why it is not your fault."

My dad, who became a Christian later in life, showed greater Christian insight than many of his theologically or psychologically educated counterparts. One day, as we were taking a walk, he asked me, "Why do you go see that shrink?"

"Well," I replied, "I guess because I want to understand why I did what I did so I can avoid doing it again."

"I can tell you that," Dad replied, catching my eye. "You did it because you wanted to."

Dad's comment goes against the grain, but it made a healthy contribution to my restoration. It drove home the truth that restoration always hinges on accepting blame and refusing to shift responsibility.

Submission versus control. Popular psychology and much of contemporary Christian thought emphasize being in control of your life and affirming your own destiny. New Age views, with their stress on the sovereignty of the individual, have permeated our thinking. Almost daily we hear people talking about the importance of boundaries and how to clearly define yourself as an individual. You must demand the respect of others and clearly delineate the influence you allow them to have on you. We are admonished to carefully place the responsibility for past hurts where it belongs and to set limits on current negative patterns of interaction. Above all, we must demonstrate without a doubt that we are in control.

How does this type of thinking go with the restoration process? Not very well! Restoration cuts against the grain here also. As a restoree, I have to face the fact that I have *not* done a good job of controlling my life. I have made bad choices; I have violated God's principles; I have damaged others; I have selfishly refused to submit to others or even consider the rights and needs of others; I have refused to submit to God and to his righteous demand that believers live holy lives; I have become hardened, arrogant and self-righteous.

Given these conditions, is the person in need of restoration in a position to control his own life and set up rules for his own healing? Of course not! Restoration is a process of guidance by which the sighted (the Spiritual Care Team) help the blind (the restoree) to repent—to walk back toward wholeness and truth.

Jack was meeting with the leader of his Spiritual Care Team. "I have three opportunities for ministry," he said, smiling confidently. After describing the offers, he asked, "What do you think?"

Recognizing that Jack was expecting his approval, the leader took a deep breath and said, "No, not yet! It will distract you too much from your main focus, which is to rebuild your relationship with God and your wife."

Jack's son was in the room during this conversation. He watched with great interest to see if his dad, previously a powerful church leader, was willing to submit. His face reflected amazement when his father said, "Okay, I can wait." And ultimately

Jack's submissive spirit not only allowed the restoration process to proceed but helped remove some hurtful barriers between him and his son.

Submission runs against the grain, but it is an essential part of restoration. The restoree needs to face the fact that he or she does not always know what is best, and the Spiritual Care Team must serve as loving, objective observers who offer input to foster growth.

Avoidance of pain versus growth. Western culture has an aversion to pain. Pain is considered bad—it is to be avoided at all costs. Dozens of medications claim to give the "fastest pain relief!" Americans spend millions of dollars annually on painkillers.

Christians have bought into the view that we shouldn't have to experience pain. We somehow believe that the good Christian will be the pain-free Christian. We practice ignoring emotional and spiritual pain with the expectation that it will go away. We use phrases like "getting beyond our mistakes," "getting on with life," "putting the past behind us." What are the implications for restoration? Avoiding pain usually results in missing many important lessons.

There are lessons to be learned from the pain that comes as a consequence of sin. One lesson is that sin is painful for the sinner *and* for all those affected. The negative impact of sin is far-reaching. The restoree needs to understand these implications in order to understand the need for confession, taking responsibility and making restitution. Restoration involves healing, and healing is almost always associated with talking through problems—with the offender taking ownership for his or her sin. This painful but essential process is what allows growth and healing to proceed.

But it takes time. We so often want instant forgiveness, instant healing and easy growth. But all of this runs counter to the biblical perspective of growing through pain and suffering. When overcoming a long and debilitating illness, the cure is worth the wait.

Misguided Notions About Forgiveness

We often assume that a sinner who asks others for forgiveness has a *right* to be forgiven—and that forgiveness must be instantaneously offered and accepted, with little regard for the pain that has been suffered. We also assume that whenever pain resurfaces, it is an indication that forgiveness has not occurred. Both are untrue.

Yes, we are to forgive others. Matthew 6:14-15 says, "If you forgive men when they sin against you, your heavenly Father will also forgive you. But if you do not forgive men their sins, your Father will not forgive your sins." But the message of these verses can be confused when the restoree *demands* forgiveness from others.

Demanding forgiveness is often a sign of nonrepentance. The repentant heart longs for forgiveness but rests in the knowledge that the only guaranteed forgiveness comes from the heavenly Father. The repentant heart prays for healing for those he or she has damaged and understands that healing takes time. He or she therefore exercises patience, longing for the day when the much-desired forgiveness will be extended. It is the responsibility of the restoree to admit doing wrong and to ask for forgiveness. Healing of relationships and forgiveness are part of God's mercy.

When I confessed my sin to my children, one of them told Sandy that he didn't think he could ever forgive me. No one pressed the issue. But in God's time healing and forgiveness came despite the level of pain and disillusionment he experienced.

The view of forgiveness that we are discussing runs against the grain. Prolonged pain indicates the degree of the hurt or injury, not the presence or absence of forgiveness. When pain comes to the surface, it reveals how severe the results of sin are; it does not mean that forgiveness has not occurred. Pain and forgiveness are different yet interrelated. Pain can continue after forgiveness. But forgiveness, honestly given in due time, can help ease that pain.

There is also a misguided notion that a person who has extended forgiveness will never speak of the offense again. Once when Sandy spoke publicly about my sin, she was told by one person that she had not forgiven me and by another that she was trying to punish me. These people believed that to talk about an offense means that you have not forgiven. In actuality, she *had* forgiven me, and this forgiveness gave both of us freedom to talk about the sin. She was emphasizing not the sin but the transformation which was occurring as a result of entering the process of restoration.

Open, nondefensive discussions promote healing and can strengthen the resolve of the offender to avoid any behavior that might add to the pain of others. Talking about pain can result in greater healing and greater trust between the offender and the one offended. When Jesus repeatedly asked Peter if he loved him, I do not think that Jesus was unforgiving. He understood forgiveness and restoration. And his honest questions furthered that process.

The distorted views presented and challenged above are deeply entrenched in the Christian community and color the way we view our world. As you read and evaluate the model of restoration presented in the chapters that follow, we hope you can expand your approach to truth and openness and find courage to go against the grain.

7

Consent for Surgery

*E*arl, *we want you* to cancel all your speaking engagements, resign from teaching at the seminary and suspend all your writing projects for at least two years. You are not in a position to be helping other people right now. You need to focus on getting your own life back together."

The question that stared me in the face that day on Catalina Island, when Paul directed me to withdraw from all of my ministry involvements, was much bigger than just "no speaking engagements." It was a question every person who has chosen a sinful path must face: *Am I willing to leave my sinful way and begin again to walk in God's light?*

I had asked for help, but was I ready to receive help in the radical form in which it was offered? As my wailing subsided that day, the choice was clear. I was being presented with a consent form for spiritual surgery. Was I going to sign it, or would I run and hide?

The need for consent and submission on the part of the restoree cannot be overemphasized. A person who has chosen to pursue sin must be willing to be carefully scrutinized and guided by others. Restorees are in no position to make independent decisions regarding their restoration. They must follow, not lead.

There may be times when the pain is so great that the restoree wants to abort the process. The path of least resistance often seems the most desirable. A few weeks into the restoration process, Virginia phoned me. We talked about some hard things. "You must not be suicidal," she said. "If you were, you surely would have chosen to escape the pain." She was right; the pain was great. As I thought about what she said, I realized that I had made the right choice: not to escape but to go forward—to face the surgery.

Consent is a very complex process, and it is not a once-and-for-all decision. The first step of consent for me was *deciding to be honest*—to stop the patterns of lying and deceit that were so ingrained. Virginia's piercing question "Have you swept the corners clean?" had to be answered honestly. With the passing of time more dirty corners came to light, revealing self-absorption, pride, disrespect for others, selfishness, mistakes in parenting, and a distorted view of my own spirituality.

A second step in the consent process is *being willing to submit to the authority of God* as revealed through the Spiritual Care Team. Jim, a fallen music minister, was directed by his Spiritual Care Team to curtail the use of his musical talents for a period of time as part of his restoration process. Not only did he lose his position at the church, but also he was required to give up additional income-producing opportunities. His Spiritual Care Team believed that the priority of restoration would be lost if Jim proceeded with business as usual. Jim reluctantly submitted and concentrated his attention on his personal growth and healing. The Spiritual Care Team released him to use his talents again, but only after time had revealed true repentance, personal healing and restored relationships.

A third aspect of giving consent is *being willing to give up secrecy.* Paul, Virginia, Larry and Nancy know more about me than they ever cared to know and certainly more than I ever intended anyone to know. Such awareness is necessary for the Spiritual Care Team to provide sound guidance and to know how and when to provide support. Secrecy is a major part of the problem. Consenting to abandon secrecy is a necessary step in the process of restoration. I believed that the worst thing in the world would be to be found out. I did everything to avoid discovery. Paradoxically, God in his wisdom revealed that discovery was exactly the thing that needed to happen to me. When I stopped hiding my sin, God was able to begin the work of restoration in me.

Consent is not really consent unless the advice of the team is actually followed. Just as medical advice is helpful only if followed, spiritual guidance must be carried out to be effective. The psalmist wrote, "When I kept silent, my bones wasted away through my groaning all day long. For day and night your hand was heavy upon me; my strength was sapped as in the heat of summer. Then I acknowledged my sin to you and did not cover up my iniquity. I said, 'I will confess my transgressions to the LORD'—and you forgave the guilt of my sin" (Ps 32:3-5). Much more than lip service is required. A person must be willing to change and to engage wholeheartedly (even though painfully) in the process.

We see the importance of being willing to change when we contrast the attitudes and outcomes of Jesus' encounters with the rich young ruler (Lk 18:18-25) and the Samaritan woman (Jn 4:4-29). Both had needs and unresolved issues. Each asked important questions. Both reached a point of having to decide what to do with the answers they received. The outcomes were drastically different. The rich young ruler would not consent to Jesus' requirements. He walked away. He chose to keep his life as it was—and lost it. The Samaritan woman was thoroughly confronted with her sin and the sinful circumstances she was living in. But her choice was different from the rich young ruler's. She chose to give up the old and embraced the process of being made over. Not only did she find life, but her choice pointed to life for many of her family and friends.

A fourth aspect of consent is *being willing to "avoid the edge"*—to break the habit of coming right up to sin and then trying to lean away just enough to keep from falling. Jane's problem was alcohol. She knew that she could not honor God with her life if she continued her drinking. She walked on the edge by not telling her friends about her problem and by going with them to restaurants and lounges where they went to drink. Even if she chose to drink just soft drinks, she was still placing herself in jeopardy. Her process of restoration was hindered by her choice to stay perched on the edge. She created continuous stress for herself and wasted massive amounts of time and energy that might have been channeled toward restoration. I too had to resolve to stay away from the things that previously had caused me to sin. I had to change my travel routes to avoid driving past nude bars and massage parlors; I had to carefully monitor what I watched on TV and what I read; I had to fastidiously avoid any area of known temptation. I couldn't afford to walk on the edge.

A Closer Look at Repentance

Giving consent for the restoration process begins with repentance. And repentance is *turning away from sin*. Saying "I'm sorry" is never enough, even if you mean it. People are often sorry or at least say so and yet choose to continue in sinful patterns. This is not repentance. Repentance involves several steps.

1. Sin must be acknowledged as sin. People rationalize, "Well, I have a little problem," or "The devil made me do it," or "I get tempted sometimes; I'm only human." They gloss over sinful choices and behaviors. I had to confess my sexual sin in its totality. I also had to say to God, Sandy, my family, the Spiritual Care Team and others, "I have lived a double life. I have been a liar and a deceiver for ten years." This acknowledgment was horribly painful, but it was an essential part of true repentance.

2. Bridges must be burned. It is not uncommon for sinners to want to take "one last look." Adulterers want to have just one more contact. Alcoholics want one last drink.

When Trevor ended his affair with Betsy and repented of his adultery, he had in his possession a number of items that belonged to Betsy. What was he to do with them?

☐ keep them until she asked for them
☐ call Betsy to see what she wanted him to do
☐ meet her at work to make the exchange
☐ ask his friend Bob to return the things to Betsy

Only the fourth answer will help Trevor successfully burn bridges. Every other option leaves open the possibility of rekindling the sinful relationship by allowing the potential for further contact. Very often, when repentance has not taken place, an individual may be remorseful and even acknowledge the sin—but be unwilling to make changes that burn bridges.

3. The possibility of sin must be ruled out. As long as the option of returning to the sin remains open in your mind, the danger of relapse is acute. Saying "I'll *try* not to repeat the sin" is not enough. This is residual behavior from an old, nonrepentant pattern. Most people who practice recurring sin have repeatedly said they were sorry and asked for forgiveness. "I'm sorry, Lord; please help me" is insufficient. A person who has ruled out sin in this way will pray, "God, I *will* not do this. I know it is a sin against you. Create in me a pure heart, O God" (Ps 51:10). He or she will also recruit help from other people in order to burn the thought-bridges to sin.

Sam, a recovering alcoholic, knows himself well. He knows

that Friday nights are a time of great temptation for him. He has ruled out a return to his sinful pattern because he recognizes that the battle is first in his mind. Having made the decision, he plans Friday nights very carefully. He tells his friends he is committed to not drinking and invites them to check up on him. He stays away from the people and places that will pull him back to his old pattern. He limits himself to safe places where the people and the atmosphere encourage him to succeed.

Scripture powerfully depicts the absurdity of returning to sin in Romans 6:21-23: "What benefit did you reap at that time from the things you are now ashamed of? Those things result in death! But now that you have been set free from sin and have become slaves to God, the benefit you reap leads to holiness, and the result is eternal life. For the wages of sin is death, but the gift of God is eternal life in Christ Jesus our Lord."

4. There must be a willingness to allow other sin to be brought to light. I was willing to admit to my sexual sin and to confess that I had deceived and lied. Wasn't that enough? No! It was only the beginning. Underlying these sins were basic patterns of self-centeredness and rebellion against God, as well as hypocrisy and a refusal to do good. All of these needed to be confessed and cleansed.

Two years into my restoration process, someone on the Spiritual Care Team said, "We're not sure that you're aware of how your sin has affected your parenting." The impact was staggering. I was rocked by a wave of defensiveness. I spent time with my kids. We sometimes had good talks. Besides, I was a recognized authority on parent-teen communication. Our family was seen as a model family. We used to go from family camp to family camp, parading our product. Now the team was suggesting that something was wrong.

With hindsight, I believe that what I was lacking was spiritual and moral leadership. When someone is in denial about his or her own moral and spiritual condition, it is impossible to lead others to a higher level. I was now being asked to face this issue head-on.

The Spiritual Care Team dared to broach this area because it was part of their job. They needed to bring to light the sins of commission and omission that were hindering God's purposes. This was one of the hardest areas for me, because it challenged my delusion that my sinful lifestyle had not negatively affected my parenting. I needed help to finally realize that sin had permeated *all* areas of my life.

Because of their commitment to full and complete restoration, the Spiritual Care Team must probe difficult areas. It is part of the surgery. It is important to remember that God's desire is full repentance from all sin.

5. Repentance needs to be understood as both an event and a lifestyle change. The event is like having a tooth pulled; the lifestyle change is like entering a total dental care program: it's a lifetime commitment. The illustration below shows God's plan for continued cleansing of the heart. It is never-ending, because we are always affected by our sinful nature.

The Cycle of Repentance

Figure 1

Repentance requires honesty, but I had not yet dealt with the patterns of deceit that had permeated my life for ten years. It came to light one day when I had an appointment to meet my friend Nate at his home.

When I arrived, Nate wasn't there. His wife said, "He must have forgotten your meeting! But he'll be back soon; feel free to wait here in the living room." I looked at my watch, realized that Nate was over fifteen minutes late, and said, "No, I'd better go. I'll just have to reschedule." I then headed for the door—only to be stopped in my tracks by the realization that this pattern was one of the ways I had covered up my past sinful behavior.

When I was stood up for a social or business engagement or finished the engagement early, I'd use the extra time to feed my sexual sin. I would call the woman with whom I was having the affair, or I'd go to a XXX-rated movie on my way back to the office. I would then justify my time to others by telling how long I had waited for an appointment who did not show, or I'd leave the time of my meeting vague. No one would question my statements. The problem was that minutes and hours were unaccounted for— time that was squandered in sinful practices.

So when I became aware of the pattern while at Nate's house, I reversed my decision and decided to wait for Nate's return. A new pattern was being formed. I reinforced this new pattern by sharing the experience with Nate as we had a late lunch. I also shared the experience with Sandy, then with Larry and later with the entire Spiritual Care Team. The process of honest disclosure is one step toward ruling out sin.

Is the Consent for Surgery Genuine?

One of the biggest concerns facing a Spiritual Care Team is how to know that the repentance is real. What indications are there that the person is genuinely committed to entering the restoration process? We acknowledge our limitations in fully knowing the heart of another person, but we do believe that certain attitudes indicate a person's lack of full commitment. The following statements call into question one's genuine "consent for surgery."

"I'm tired of dealing with all this pain." Restoration is a very painful process, because sin brings painful consequences. A common sentiment of the person being restored is "I feel like I'm being peeled like an onion. Each layer reveals someone else I have hurt, something else I've done wrong or one more consequence I have to face." Constantly confronting your sinful past really hurts. The fact is, however, there is no other path through restoration. To avoid the pain is to avoid the process and thus thwart God's mercy and healing. When a person is willing to learn from pain and sorrow, cleansing and healing result.

The apostle Paul's words to the believers in Corinth illustrate this process: "Even if I caused you sorrow by my letter, I do not regret it. . . . I see that my letter hurt you, but only for a little while—yet now I am happy, not because you were made sorry, but because your sorrow led you to repentance. For you became sorrowful as God intended and so were not harmed in any way by us. Godly sorrow brings repentance that leads to salvation and leaves no regret, but worldly sorrow brings death" (2 Cor 7:8-10).

Paul did not regret having brought sorrow to the people of Corinth when he confronted them about their sin, because he knew that God uses sorrow to bring about repentance and healing.

"I'm not the only sinner here." It's easy to excuse my own sinfulness by comparison with others. In an attempt to take the spotlight off my guilt, I may blame someone else or call attention to the fact that everyone sins. But God does not judge by comparison. He is not asking me to focus on other people's sins; it's *my* sin that God wants me to face and confess. Then God will forgive and cleanse me.

"I just want to get on with my life." This phrase is very popular. And it sounds good! However, it is very dangerous if unexamined.

It may be used as an excuse for lack of repentance, incomplete repentance or refusal to deal with the consequences of sin. I asked my therapist one day, "When is this going to be over?" He replied with one word: "Never!" As hard as this may be to hear, it is *brutally* true. Sin irrevocably changes our lives. The consequences of past sinful choices are forever woven into the fabric of one's life. They destroy opportunities and force major adjustments. Repentance involves change and newness of life, but part of the new life may be to delve into the consequences of past choices. The Spiritual Care Team must make sure the process is completed. Not to do so may allow the sinner to avoid dealing fully with the real issues. Anything less than a thorough job will short-circuit the effectiveness of the process.

Medical surgery is always accompanied by elements of risk and a certain number of unknowns. Even so, a patient will consent to the operation because the potential for health and wholeness is more important than the risks attached.

So it is with the ministry of restoration. When we are in need of spiritual surgery, we "sign" the consent form knowing that there are inherent risks and plenty of unknowns. We sign it regardless, because we are convinced that apart from this painful process we will never experience health and wholeness as God intended.

8

Truth *and* Consequences

*W**hen Sandy and I went** to Catalina to talk with the Friesens that painful October weekend, one of the questions that came up repeatedly was "Who really needs to know, and how much needs to be disclosed?"

In the ensuing days and months, many other hard questions related to disclosure arose. Should a formal statement be sent out? If so, how would it be disseminated? What would it say? Did the whole story need to be told? Should those at church be told? If so, how should they be told?

Should I tell my clients? I'd risk losing significant income and the trust these people had vested in me. Would their lives be even more confused by this information? Should we tell our children? Wouldn't it be better to spare them the pain and disappointment in their father? Should I tell my aging father? Wouldn't it be kinder to let my father die believing his son was a "success"? What about those at the seminary? Would I lose my teaching position if I was totally honest with them?

The questions we posed are not unique to my situation. Similar questions must be asked by anyone who takes seriously the truth of James 5:16, which instructs us to "confess [our] sins to each other." The need for confession is clear. The question of how widely the confession should extend must be sensitively explored.

The Evolution of Secret-Keeping

The early church practiced openness in their confession of sins. Believers followed the admonition to confess their sins to one another. Implicit in this instruction is face-to-face interaction. Matthew 18:15-17 says, "If your brother sins against you, go and show him his fault, just between the two of you. If he listens to you, you have won your brother over. But if he will not listen, take one or two others along, so that 'every matter may be established by the testimony of two or three witnesses.' If he refuses to listen to them, tell it to the church; and if he refuses to listen even to the church, treat him as you would a pagan or a tax collector." The clear instruction is to deal with another's sin not by going behind the person's back but by meeting the person face to face. If this does not bring about change, the next step is to take another witness or two along, and, if no repentance occurs, the final step is to take the matter before the church.

Matthew 5:23-24 reminds us of the importance of reconciliation: "Therefore, if you are offering your gift at the altar and there remember that your brother has something against you, leave your gift there in front of the altar. First go and be reconciled to your brother; then come and offer your gift."

In *Physicians of the Soul*, Charles Kemp states, "The indications of all the early literature are that confession in the first centuries was public. In fact, the clergy opposed private confession and insisted that sins confessed in private should be made known publicly. This included all sins, both those sins committed in secret and those already known to the public (New York: Macmillan, 1947, p. 26).

In the Roman Catholic Church, sins were to be confessed to the priest, thus alleviating the need to confess to other people. At the time of the Reformation, Martin Luther said that Christians were able to confess their sins to God and God alone. Today most Protestants continue in this practice of going not to our brothers and sisters but to God alone.

However, we may be missing something. Dietrich Bonhoeffer comments on the value of confessing to other people: "Since the confession of sin is made in the presence of a Christian brother, the last stronghold of self-justification is abandoned. The sinner surrenders; he gives up all his evil. He gives his heart to God, and he finds the forgiveness of all his sin in the fellowship of Jesus Christ and his brother" (*Life Together* [New York: Harper & Row, 1954], p. 112).

For a person struggling with an addiction, the practice of confession to God alone and not to fellow believers can contribute to a life of isolation and secrecy.

The Problem with Secret-Keeping

I sought advice from a pastor friend regarding the extent of my confession. He told me to not disclose anything to the church. He also advised me not to share any more details with Sandy. On the one hand, I was relieved by this advice; I didn't want to hurt anyone. I didn't want to face the consequences of my sinfulness. Continuing to keep secrets was very appealing. On the other hand, something within me said, *This isn't right.*

Secret-keeping allows the person to perpetuate sinful patterns. It also facilitates the sinner's denial about the full extent of the sin and its impact. The choice to be a secret-keeper prevents healing in the individual, the family and the church. Family and church members may be aware that something is wrong, but they're not sure what that might be. They receive both direct and indirect messages that they are not to ask. So they often withdraw, leaving the sinner alone with his or her secrets. The sinner suppresses the pain and thus hinders any prospect of healing.

Secret-keeping has its roots in the Garden of Eden. Adam and Eve chose to hide from God, thinking their sin would not be found out. This pattern of hiding was set in motion and is in the fabric of who we are as fallen people. We rationalize our hiding with thoughts such as *I don't want to hurt my spouse; it's no one else's business; everyone has their "closet sins."* The truth is that self-protection is our motivation for hiding. We don't want to be hurt, shamed, judged or embarrassed; we don't want to suffer loss of respect. Scripture warns us against such secrecy and self-protectiveness: "He who conceals his sins does not prosper, but whoever confesses and renounces them finds mercy" (Prov 28:13).

Encouraging secrecy misses God's carefully designed plan for life within the body of Christ. James 5:16 tells us, "Confess your sins to each other and pray for each other so that you may be healed. The prayer of a righteous man is powerful and effective." Confession to God and to each other is required, and it includes prayer and forgiveness. None of this can happen within the context of secret-keeping. Rather, secret-keeping renders the body of Christ impotent to fulfill its responsibility to each member when it comes to dealing with temptation and sin.

The Impact of Dishonesty

A wise friend, in teaching on the value of truth-telling versus lying, pointed out that "God is not limited by our weaknesses; he is limited by our dishonesty." This same principle applies to honesty within other relationships. Although confession of sin and weakness will bring pain to our families, friends and churches, it provides the opportunity to deal with the sin. Dishonesty, on the other hand, makes it impossible to work with the issues surrounding the sin. Individuals and congregations remain immobilized by secret sins. The health of the body of Christ is compromised by dishonesty.

During one of our team discussions, Nancy told us about the devastation she felt when it was announced in church that her pastor, whom she liked and respected, had suddenly and inexplicably resigned. The congregation feared the worst but sat in stunned silence. In the aftermath of the announcement, no one dared to ask why he had resigned, and no explanations were forthcoming. The pastor left town without any further contact with church members, so no healthy closure was possible. Gossip and misunderstanding spread. Disillusioned people left the church. Folks were confused, and they were left with no one to turn to. Nancy's emotions ranged from anger and betrayal to abandonment and loss. Secrecy proved to be deadly, choking out spiritual vitality and preventing restoration and healing within the congregation.

The choice to be honest and tell the truth about yourself and your sin has broad implications. Honesty sets in motion a cycle of events and attitudes that affect both the truth-teller and all those around him or her. Dishonesty has far-reaching implications as well and sets in motion a cycle of its own. Compare the two cycles as conceptualized on page 78.

These diagrams show that choices to be honest lead to growth, healing and expanded positive possibilities for the truth-teller. Choices to be dishonest, on the other hand, lead to reduced possibilities for personal healing and growth. The choice to be honest is a life-changing, life-giving choice.

When Dr. McIvor asked me if I had told my dad about the things I had done, I said, "No. He's old and about to die; why would I want to tell him this stuff?"

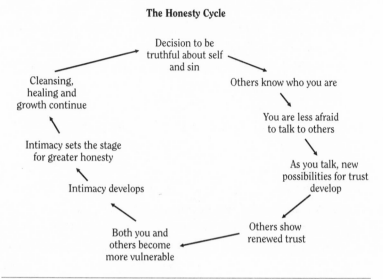

Figure 2

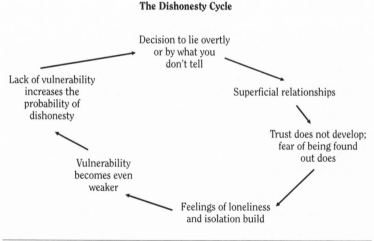

Figure 3

Dr. McIvor's reply was piercing. "It depends on what kind of relationship you want to have with him while he is living. If you want a superficial relationship based on more lies and deceit, then don't tell him. On the other hand, if you want a close and open relationship with him, then you'll need to tell him. He may even have wisdom from which you can benefit."

After I decided to tell Dad and my stepmom, the wisdom of those words became apparent. Dad did give me helpful input. And because I no longer had to cover up, I found myself able to spend more time with him. After making the long drive to keep a counseling appointment, I could stop in the nearby city where Dad was in a nursing home and take him out for a meal.

One day, when Sandy and I took him back to the nursing home, he said, "Do you know what the guys who live here call my room?"

"No; what do they call it?"

"They call it Envy Hotel. Everyone in here is envious of me because I have someone who comes to take me out for meals. I have someone who cares."

If I had not told Dad the truth, I would have stayed away for fear of having to explain why I was in the neighborhood so regularly—and all of that would have been lost.

A false dichotomy has developed within the community of believers regarding honesty. Our thinking has become distorted: we believe that it is impossible to be loving and forgiving and at the same time to be honest. Honesty is associated with pain and hurt—and those things are seen as opposites of love and forgiveness. We wrongly believe that to love or forgive means never bringing sinful realities into focus since they would result in pain. Such thinking is dangerous and debilitating; it avoids pain at the expense of healing.

The Biblical Directive

Ephesians 4:25 tells us, "Each of you must put off falsehood and speak truthfully to his neighbor, for we are all members of one body." The directives of this verse are first, not to lie, and second, to speak truth.

Lying is an acceptable behavior in our culture. "White lies" are considered benign. In a recent counseling session Paul and Virginia were conducting with a couple, the husband stated that it was fine to lie to his wife about little things if telling her the truth would hurt her feelings. He gave as an example stopping for a beer on the way home from work, a practice his wife did not approve of. To excuse his lateness he would tell her that he had had to work late, because he knew that the truth would upset her. He rationalized that this was the loving thing to do. Paul asked him at what point the truth would be the right choice—for instance, if he were to commit adultery, would it be acceptable to continue his pattern of lying since the truth would hurt her?

"Of course I'd tell her the truth about that; that's a big issue!" he responded.

Skepticism crept into Paul's voice as he asked, "So you would lie to your wife about drinking a couple of beers to avoid hurting her feelings, but you would tell her about an affair?" The husband nodded yes. (It later turned out that he *was* having an affair at the time when he made those statements!)

Once we justify lying in order not to hurt someone, we've opened the door to speaking truth only when convenient and comfortable. Lying becomes acceptable and justifiable. The obvious problem is that this sort of thinking runs contrary to the biblical mandate to not speak falsehoods, and therefore it is sin.

The second part of the verse instructs us to speak truthfully. Speaking truthfully goes a step beyond not lying. Speaking truthfully requires that we tell whole truths, not half-truths. It requires that we reveal the whole story, not just the parts that will benefit or protect us. Speaking truthfully is a commitment to being honest and being known, as opposed to being secretive or deceptive. This verse instructs us not to lie—by commission or by omission. Both are equally wrong. Ultimately we must be convinced that truth is life-giving and falsehood is life-robbing. Even when the truth hurts, it opens the path to life. This is foundational if restoration is to occur.

Applying the Honesty Principle

Scripture mandates that we must practice honesty and confess sins. Does that mean that each sin of each church member must be publicly confessed each Sunday? Just how extensively should the truth be told? How far should the circle of confession extend?

The repentant individual must make a commitment to telling the truth when asked about rumors or otherwise questioned about past behavior. Anything less smacks of a cover-up and will further undermine the credibility of the individual and the Christian community. When the honesty principle is applied, there is an opportunity for both believers and unbelievers to encourage the individual's progress in restoration and to see the faithfulness of God being lavished on the one who honestly and fully repents. Unbelievers will be more convinced of the veracity of the gospel by seeing grace and mercy applied to the life of the repentant fallen believer than by seeing a sinner deceitfully hiding behind claims of perfection or denying a sin that others believe to exist.

People will always be hurt by honest revelations. The source of the hurt, however, is not in the telling but in the sin itself. Not telling only compounds the hurt. Further, we disagree with Scripture if we say, "No one will know; it will soon blow over." Numbers 32:23 warns us, "Be sure that your sin will find you out."

Secrecy Causes Problems

Such openness is not often practiced in the Christian community. Commonly, a statement is issued by the elders or some other governing board that reads something like this: "Due to personal reasons, Pastor S_____ has resigned." Because confusion and contradiction usually surround such an event, the lack of truth breeds rumors and gossip (more sin), and the congregation is hurt. Innocent parishioners may feel rejected or abandoned—not only by the offender but even more by the actions of their leaders. In contrast, the congregation that hears a complete confession (complete in nature, not in gory detail) from their pastor will be free from speculation regarding the truth and able to move forward in praying for restoration through discipline. The church has the opportunity to grow from the hurt and pain rather than muddle around in the quagmire produced by secrecy, confusion, speculation and rumor.

George was the pastor of a small church. When it was disclosed to an elder by a member of the church that the pastor had sexually molested her, George was fired. The congregation was told that the pastor was being let go for personal reasons, but word leaked out that the personal reason was sexual impropriety. The rumors flew, ranging from speculation of an affair he had had sixteen years ago to guesses about who might be the present victim. The church was wracked by rumors and gossip due to lack of honest disclosure. It would have been much better to deal with the truth up front and to promote healing among those who were dealing with feelings of betrayal and confusion instead of leaving many with deep wounds and spiritual disillusionment.

The church rationalized withholding the truth about the pastor as "protecting" the victim. They felt that if full disclosure were made, the congregation would figure out the identity of the victim, which would only increase her pain. What happened instead is that the pastor's discipline and restoration were derailed due to lack of honest confession, and the victim was forced to keep hiding, which prevented her healing. She became an unattended casualty.

The congregation continued to be confused, hurt, angry and abandoned. The church leaders ignored the principle that healing for the offender, the victim and the congregation can begin only when the truth is spoken. The leaders would have served the church body biblically and with integrity had they issued a statement such as "Because Pastor George has had a history of sexual offenses and has continued to violate individuals recently, he has been removed from the pulpit for a time of repentance, discipline, therapy and restoration. He has agreed to answer all questions and wishes to apologize publicly to all who wish to attend a meeting set for next Sunday night at 7:00."

We are aware of more than one case in which pastors have been let go because of immoral behavior and the church has agreed to keep the situation secret so as to not threaten their employability. The thinking goes like this: "We're going to have to let you go, but we won't mention anything about your offense so you can get a 'fresh start' somewhere else."

Such reasoning is very unfair to churches that are calling a new pastor. And, despite seemingly good intentions, it is unfair to the pastor and his family. The pastor's best interests are not served because he is not forced to face his failure or is not helped with restoration. In most of these situations, instead of a "fresh start" it becomes simply a continuation of previous moral failures. No one can learn, grow and start over with the merciful, corrective help of the heavenly Father when secrecy prevails. Truth-telling honors the person's church, friends and family; covering up does not.

Our team summarized it this way:

For the offender seeking restoration, full disclosure of sin is critical if healing is to come. The facts need to be told. Not the personal gory details, but enough information so that the audience knows what the actual offense was. In Earl's situation, it was not enough to say that he had committed adultery (though that was true). The whole truth was that he was a sexual addict, and that involved not only adultery, but also massage parlors, prostitutes, nude bars and pornography. To withhold the nature of the offense because "it might hurt others" is often a smokescreen to avoid exposure. It also serves to encourage denial and incomplete repentance on the part of the offender.

In my case, the Spiritual Care Team helped me decide how to admit *all* of this behavior to the broad spectrum of people in my life. Disclosure was handled in different ways with different individuals or groups of people.

☐ I spoke directly to each of our children (ages fifteen to twenty-five at the time). I told them everything.

☐ I spoke directly to our parents and family members.

☐ I confessed face to face to our new pastor.

☐ I publicly confessed to the elders at our church.

☐ I had personal conversations, some by phone and some face to face, with close friends and colleagues.

☐ Once I was released to take speaking engagements again, I disclosed to those who invited me to speak. (The team encouraged me to answer all questions straightforwardly and without self-protection.)

☐ I disclosed by letter to the professional licensing board.

☐ I disclosed to my current clients.

☐ I met with the governing board of one of the camps I had worked with significantly over the years and fully disclosed to them.

☐ I sent a letter of confession to my colleagues at the seminary.

The team helped me be committed to truth-telling. They helped me see that, regardless of how tired I got of telling the story, regardless of whether I felt that I had been open enough and shouldn't have to keep bringing up the sordid truth of my past, part of the consequence of my sin was that in some ways it would always be with me. I couldn't afford to lapse into deception or covering up; I would always need to be open to answering questions. Just recently I ran into an acquaintance whom I hadn't seen for years. Intuiting from his questions that he had heard something but didn't have many facts, I invited him to lunch and proceeded to explain what God had done in my life in the past seven years. He expressed great appreciation for my openness and for the restorative work of God.

Satan is the father of lies and uses deception as one of his most effective weapons. He deceives us into believing that lying by omission is less damaging than lying by commission (or even benign). He gets as much mileage as possible out of the lying done within the body of Christ.

Withholding the truth because it may hurt someone eventually hurts many more people, stifles growth and usually spawns more lies. Lies are needed to cover up lies. Thus an endless cycle of sinful deception is created. If we buy the lie that it is better to be silent or even tell a lie than to hurt somebody, we avoid ever having to reveal anything that might embarrass us, because very likely any such revelation will hurt *someone*. We should have thought of that before we committed the offense! Only the truth can break the cycle of deception and pave the way for restoration and healing.

Truth-Telling and the Victim

Should the offender's sin be told when an innocent victim's name will be revealed as part of the story? Where sexual sins are involved, victims are often branded as co-conspirators. It is sometimes suggested that "she must have asked for it" or "he must not have met her emotional needs." This type of inaccurate reasoning must be exposed. Many people have been victimized by others' sinful choices. Victims should be comforted, affirmed and encouraged by all who know them and understand what has happened. This is impossible when secrecy is the rule and people hear only rumors. Those in places of leadership need to discuss the importance of truth with a victim. For the victim as well as the offender, truth ultimately is far less damaging than living with rumor or with the fear of being found out.

God's people need to look their brothers or sisters in the eye and say, "I'm really sorry that it was another brother who hurt you so badly. It should never have happened. We want to assist you in your healing." Secrecy designed to protect the victim may end up hurting the victim more or denying the victim this assistance in healing.

When believers within one congregation or one community sin against one another, the nature of the sin should be made known. The sinner should be encouraged in repentance, restitution and restoration, while the victim should be accepted, encouraged in healing, ministered to and affirmed in the process of forgiveness.

Disclosure of the victim's identity should be done only with the victim's approval. The reasons for truth-telling can be discussed with them, and they should be assured that a group of believers will surround them with love and help them work through the pain. Rumors usually leak the victim's identity; however, rumors are often half-truths or embellishments of the worst kind. Once the facts are told, false rumors can die and our efforts can turn to comfort and healing.

In situations where there has been consensual involvement, both parties need to confess and be restored. In cases where there has been a misuse of power, such as when someone is encouraged to participate in sin by a person in authority (a psychologist, pastor, counselor, teacher, youth leader, church leader), the person in the authority position must always be held primarily responsible. Victims, however, should be helped to evaluate their involvement and accept responsibility for their own choices. Sharing responsibility does not mean taking the heat off the person in authority. Each person must claim full responsibility for the level of sinful choices he or she has made.

Truth-Telling and the Family

Full disclosure is terribly embarrassing for the family members of the one following a sinful path. All pretenses come crashing down. Family members realize that they have been deceived and lied to. They do not want others to know. They don't want to see their family member disgraced. They don't want to experience shame and disgrace themselves. On the other hand, they are sick of lies and fully aware of the destruction that dishonesty has brought to their family. A battle wages inside. If the truth is told, how can family members avoid the pain? If the truth is suppressed, how can they ever trust again or hope to heal?

One of the real anxieties for Sandy and the children was the details of my unfaithfulness. The need to know went hand in hand with the sense of betrayal. Sandy didn't know how to stop her mental questions: *When did all this happen? What were the details? How often did it take place?* The Spiritual Care Team can help the spouse work through his or her need to know these details. The little things in the tumultuous reconstruction process become important and must be dealt with in one fashion or another. When some painful disclosure has to be made to answer the questions, the pain should be acknowledged and dealt with as the facts emerge.

Covering up the truth to protect loved ones will send the wrong message to family members and all others who are watching. It says, "You can't face the truth; it hurts too much." It also denies the biblical emphasis of telling the truth. In choosing to make the entire story public, we demonstrate a belief that God is the only protector we have. He will honor a faith that says publicly, "This is what I did. It was dreadfully wrong and it hurt many people, including my family. I denounce this wrong and pledge myself once again to God and to my family. They did not commit these sins; I did. They are not guilty; I am. Please treat them with kindness and encouragement as they struggle to stabilize their faith in God and their trust in me."

One of my daughters and I were invited to the home of some family friends, Debbie and John. After dinner John said to my daughter, "How are you doing regarding all the things your dad did? It must be hard when the one who has represented God to you turns out to have lied, broken his marriage vows and done things he often spoke against."

Tears flowed freely, and for the next hour I listened in broken amazement as God used John and Debbie to minister to my daughter, who had been crushed and confused by my actions. As the conversation ended and John and Debbie carried dishes into the kitchen, my daughter said, "Daddy, I've forgiven you, and I don't hate you, but it just hurts so bad."

Without truth these much-needed healing moments will not likely occur. Debbie and John took the risk of becoming involved and became ministers of God's mercy. They were able to do so because the truth had been told.

Truth-Telling and the Church and Community

About nine months into the therapy process, Dr. McIvor, my therapist, made a notation in my journal next to an entry where I had questioned whether I would ever be respected again. He wrote, "Men stand tall with truth."

About a month later I went to a meeting of my church's elder board to make a full confession. As I drove there, I felt shame and worthlessness. After I finished talking, one of the elders gave me a bear hug, looked me in the eye and said, "You're a very tall man to me right now." Tears of joy and gratitude swept over me like a warm shower. Truth and respect go together.

Other people have told me that it has been important for them to know about my restoration process as a means of growing spiritually themselves. One said, "I don't ever want to do what you have done, but you are showing us how important it is to face the truth."

Public awareness of sin, accompanied by awareness of the mercy of God and his people in restoring the sinner, is an important testimony to how God deals with sin and human failure. Both God's people and nonbelievers need to know that God requires repentance—and that repentance leads to healing and renewal for the wounded spirit. What better way for an unbeliever to see God's great love and his willingness to forgive and receive all who come to him in faith?

Unbelievers can also benefit from seeing the way the church rallies behind the repentant person and nurtures him or her back into the family of God. The story of the prodigal son bears repeating each time a wayward one responds to the discipline of God and returns to God the Father and to his family. People separated from God need to know how God treats wayward children who repent. It's good news!

Truth-Telling and the Spiritual Care Team

Honesty leads to trust, vulnerability, intimacy and growth. I've been told that my growing willingness to deal truthfully with my sin affected the team in a contagious way. We all became more truthful, more willing to become honest with each other and with God. Nancy recalls one experience:

Earl brought his journal to one meeting and read the comments Dr. McIvor had written across the pages regarding truth. Some of those comments were "You're shifting responsibility," "avoidance of truth," "trickle-down truth-telling," "trying to hide," "selective disclosure," "You're using benevolence (not wanting to hurt others) as an excuse for lying and not facing the truth." The list went on. It seemed that I was guilty of all those comments as well. My discomfort increased. It was difficult to focus on Earl and Sandy as I pondered my own life. I was being refined.

The topic of discussion that day was truthful communication in marriage. This was stuff that hit very close to home—so close that by the close of our meeting, we were making remarks about the similarity of each couple's situation. Larry and I drove home in silence. I wondered if he was doing the deep personal evaluation this meeting had caused me to do. Holes in our marriage were revealed as I observed Earl and Sandy's tenacious endeavor to revive their shattered relationship.

My stomach knotted and churned as I watched them work through complex problems. Could I be as transparent and honest about our marriage as Earl and Sandy had been? Did I *want* to be? *Give me determination, Lord,* I prayed. I know marriage improvement is a lifelong process. Could I respond to the uneasiness I was feeling in an honest and godly way?

I realized that this restoration team had something to offer all of us. Today I was being offered home improvement. This meeting had not been just a place for me to sit in the bleachers and cheer the Wilsons on. I had an opportunity to get in the game!

We still had a twenty-minute drive before we would get home. There was plenty of time to talk. I looked over at my husband and broke the silence by tossing a question at him: "Could you see any similarities between our relationship and Earl and Sandy's struggles?"

Larry didn't take his eyes off the road, but his body tensed in defense. A long pause preceded his cautious answer: "Well, perhaps . . ."

I sensed his openness, so I asked, "What did you think of Dr. McIvor's definitions of the ways people lie? Are we missing some things?"

For a while our conversation became a scrimmage as we analyzed difficult areas of communication in our relationship. As we talked, we became more honest—without adding a spiteful tone to our comments. The meeting had prompted us to work toward deeper levels of truth in problem areas. In fact, truth-telling and honesty had a contagious, positive effect on the whole team. We were all prompted to take the tools we were pressing the Wilsons to apply and use them in our own relationships with spouse, family and friends.

Without truth-telling there is no basis for approaching God. Without freedom to approach God there is no restoration for sinner, victim, family, church or community. Without restoration there is no healing and no hope. With truth-telling the positive consequences far outweigh the negative. Jesus, who is the Truth, sets us free from sin.

9

What About the Spouse & Family?

The team asked Sandy to write this chapter, looking back at the whole process from her own perspective—both at how she reacted to the crisis and at what sources of help were most meaningful.

*A*s *I drink in the beauty* of this crisp fall day, I am awed that I feel so at peace and so thankful for my life. Seven years ago, when my world shattered through the revelation of my husband's unfaithfulness, no one could have convinced me that I would ever celebrate life again.

Although I had had suspicions of Earl's infidelity in years past, I had always repressed them. The letter I held in my hand that Sunday in October 1989 confirmed what I had believed deep down but had not wanted to know: he had had an affair with a former client whom I knew. Numbness swept over me as the truth of those words sunk in. Robotically I went through the motions needed to carry on life over the next day and a half. I even assured

Earl that we would get through this.

Sleep eluded me Monday night. In my restlessness, I got up to try to make sense of what was happening in my world by writing. My feelings spilled out on the paper. Angry words connected feelings of panic, uncertainty, confusion, hurt, pain and a plethora of other emotions. I wrote through the night. As dawn approached, a plan began to formulate in my mind: I would arrange to have dinner with Earl Thursday evening, at which time I would tell him that I was leaving. At first I had said I would stay, but I knew I couldn't. I couldn't imagine any solution other than leaving him.

Numbly I went through the next days. Pain immobilized me from doing anything but what was necessary for survival. When Thursday evening arrived, Earl and I went out to dinner. I needed to be out of our home when I gave him my decision.

Earl appeared crushed, frantic about my choice to leave. He begged me to change my mind. Although I felt resolute about my decision, I agreed to reconsider while I was gone for the weekend speaking at a previously scheduled retreat.

After the conference ended that weekend, I stole away to the beach to process the decision hanging over my head. I sat on a bench and prayed in my numbed state. Although everything in my world seemed to be spinning out of control, I still had confidence in the steadfastness of God—and I turned to him for help and guidance. Gradually I sensed that God was leading me to stay and work on things, at least for a while. With that assurance, I began the long drive home. Questions swirled through my mind during the two-hour drive, but no answers surfaced. The numbness continued. I was so overwhelmed by the magnitude of this crisis in our lives that I did not know how I would survive.

When I got home, I told Earl that I had decided to stay for now. I was flooded with a sense of relief that this decision was made, and I began to focus on what needed to happen to make it stick. I asked Earl to flesh out his promise to change by agreeing to several requests: that he would see a therapist; that we would seek outside input regarding our future speaking commitments; that he would completely sever ties with the other woman. We had taken the first tentative steps down a path I had never expected to travel.

It was clear to me that we could not walk down this path alone. Earl's mind, however was racing to figure out the simplest way for life to return to normal. He wanted to "fix it" on his own. I was disgusted by his thinking and knew it was flawed. I pushed for reaching out to someone else who could help us through these dark days. The Spiritual Care Team was born out of this need.

I also needed some close friends to come around me on a daily basis. I needed someone to listen, to validate my pain, to pray for me, to tell me Earl's choices were not my fault, to let me vent my anger and frustration, to help me make practical decisions. The three women friends I invited to enter my shattered world fleshed out Jesus' love to me consistently and faithfully over the next several years. Each one in her own unique way was there for me.

I remember one occasion when I felt overwhelmed by discouragement. One of those friends just held me for a long time. She gave me no answers, she made no promises, she just helped me feel love and comfort. Somehow her love instilled hope in me and broke through my despair.

These friends (and several couples in whom we confided and who stuck by us) became even more important after Earl's sin became public and I was abandoned by a number of other friends and colleagues. Some people rallied to support Earl, who was open about his brokenness and devastation, but they seemed clueless about my needs and even avoided me. Some blamed me for Earl's choices. Still others vented their anger toward Earl by telling me how they felt but refusing to confront Earl. This created even more anger and confusion within me. But the rejection and insensitivity I experienced at times was offset by the lovingkindness of my faithful friends. They were also invaluable in reaffirming my worth as a person and rebuilding my shattered self-esteem. The role of friends like these in the aftermath of such brokenness cannot be underestimated.

The Spouse's Need for Opposite-Sex Support

The Spiritual Care Team met a different sort of need from what could be met by my women friends. I realized I also needed male perspective. My father was dead, I had no brothers, I was without a pastor—and the primary male in my life had totally betrayed me. Over the years I had allowed Earl to intimidate, invalidate and discount me in his attempt to cover up his secret life.

Over the years I had felt that we had a better-than-average marriage, but there was something wrong. A negative pattern had developed in our relationship. I would state my opinions or express my feelings—and Earl would counter them. He spoke firmly and usually defensively. I would eventually back off to keep peace. I couldn't understand why I was always wrong or why I felt so alone. This form of interaction fed into my flagging self-esteem.

So now the possibility of restoring the marriage seemed overwhelming and frightening. How could we deal with our conflicts with this present destructive pattern of communicating? I realized how wrong Earl was, but how could I tell him? He hadn't listened to me in the past—why would things be any different now? I needed help. I felt a need for male perspective in a safe atmosphere.

As the Spiritual Care Team formed, Larry and Paul began to fulfill that need. Although they were supporting Earl in his walk down the road of repentance, they did not allow him to take shortcuts that would be hurtful to me or the rest of the family. They also strengthened me when I started standing up against the shortcuts that Earl sometimes proposed. There was open communication between me and the other members. The team members avoided taking sides; they were straightforward and open with all parties.

During the early Spiritual Care Team meetings, I felt uncertain that Larry could or would be helpful to me because of his loyalty to Earl. We discussed the issue openly in the meeting and between the two of us until a positive bond was formed. By the time the discussions were over, Larry's usefulness in the process was enhanced by his ability to relate in a confrontative or supportive way to both Earl and me. This would not have taken place if I had not aired my feelings and if Larry had not been willing to listen. The team validated over and over again how important my input was in helping to guide the restoration process.

During the early stages, Earl did not know what was best for him. (The same is true of most restorees.) He desperately wanted a return to the familiar—he wanted to get things back to "normal" rather than face the hard steps of change. There were some things that I thought needed to happen but that, without the support of the team—especially the male members—I would have been reluctant to push for.

For example, I was the one who first brought up the necessity for Earl to withdraw from public ministry. Earl resisted. It was Paul who directed Earl to give up speaking and writing. I knew it should happen, but I had to have the support and authority of the others to back me up. It was the group, with Paul leading, who told Earl that he should not work for a year. I did not know how to stand up against Earl by myself, and so I needed this help from the others. I gained insights into myself and into Earl each time we met with the Spiritual Care Team.

Earl's therapist, Dr. McIvor, also served to provide a positive male perspective, which was helpful to me. Early in the process I had a session with Dr. McIvor during which he helped me deal with the issue of responsibility. He helped me realize that regardless of the circumstances that had contributed to Earl's behavior, he could have made other choices—and that I was in no way responsible for the choices he had made. He helped me to see that it was Earl's sinful decisions that had brought the marriage to the brink of destruction. Dr. McIvor's support protected me from placing the blame on myself. He also helped me to understand that Earl's style of relating was deceitful, accusatory and intimidating. I began to learn how to stand up to Earl rather than acquiesce to his intimidation.

Later in the recovery process, Dr. McIvor helped me to take a careful look at areas in our relationship that were unhealthy. These unhealthy patterns had not caused the adultery, but needed to be changed in order for us to experience health in our marriage, now that it was no longer threatened by the adulterous relationship.

It helped me to have both male and female perspectives during the restoration process. It was very important to have opposite-sex support in a safe environment. Within the context of the Spiritual Care Team the danger of compromise or inappropriate emotional involvement was greatly reduced. It was helpful to me that the team was made up of both men and women and that I was able to glean support in a context where goals, purposes and expectations were kept clear.

The Ministry of Same-Sex Team Members

I desperately wanted two things from the supportive relationships in my life during this crisis. First, I wanted my friends to make the pain go away. Second, I wanted them to tell me what to do. I came to realize they could do neither. They could be with me in my pain, but I had to be the one who worked through it. Pain is a guaranteed byproduct of such a broken-world experience, and no one could remove it for me. Neither could anyone make my decisions for me. They could give me counsel and input, but ultimately I needed to choose my own path.

I had many women friends, and they cared for me in a variety of ways. Although I would not have called Nancy or Virginia intimate friends prior to our team experience, they certainly became intimate friends during the process of restoration. They ministered to me in myriad ways during this time. They helped me keep some perspective during the whole healing process. They invested huge amounts of their time and energy. They fit me into already overfull schedules. They prayed for me; I was very aware of that. They sent cards and letters. They called me and listened to my anger, pain, discouragement or whatever. They consistently were available to me whenever a need arose. Compassion, commitment and continuity describe well their involvement in my life.

Each of them ministered to me in broad and specific ways that reflected their individual giftedness. I highlight these specifics to demonstrate how God uses the unique gifts and personalities of each Spiritual Care Team member. Nancy brought the gift of prayer to the team and was a special help to me and to Earl because she did not just *say* she would pray; she prayed. She was very specific about our prayer needs and regularly checked to see how God was answering prayer. Nancy encouraged me by challenging Earl in his prayer life, which the team recognized was weak. Her strong gift of hospitality also nurtured each of us on the team as she created special times and events that made us feel loved and cared for.

In a powerful yet humble way, Virginia used her strong gift of discernment for me as well as for Earl. She allowed God to use her to question thoughts and feelings in a very straightforward but unassuming manner. Virginia was very sensitive to the pain I was experiencing regarding our children. I felt loved because I knew of Virginia's love and concern for the children. I was cared for tangibly by all of the team members as they put love into action on my behalf, consistently, sacrificially and sensitively.

It was very difficult for me to share my fears and concerns for Earl with Earl himself. I didn't want to discourage him, and I didn't want the healing process to be aborted. I needed regular encouragement from Dr. McIvor and the Spiritual Care Team in order to confront the issues that were important to Earl's progress and the restoration of our marriage.

Did the team always meet every need, hurt or pain? No, they didn't. Although I wanted them to, they could not, nor could any team. I experienced times of feeling let down or disappointed by them. Yet as I reflect on their role in our recovery, I am overwhelmed by their faithful, steady investment in us. I have a deeper awareness that only God can truly meet my needs, heal my pain and lift me above my hurt. The team fleshed out God's love to me to the greatest extent that any group of humans could as they worked together in a powerful way on our behalf.

Working Toward Marital Restoration

Restoration is a lengthy process. We went through several different phases: denial or avoidance of the problem, fatigue and depression, growth, setbacks, and more growth. Thoughts and emotions came and went in waves; anger, bitterness, loneliness and rejection rode the crest.

If marital restoration is to become a reality, it must be carefully nurtured. During our process, several key elements emerged.

Honesty is the foundational issue for marital restoration. Until Earl was willing to commit himself to truth-telling, there was no basis for rebuilding the marriage. Trust cannot develop in the absence of honesty. Restorees are not inclined to tell the truth, the whole truth and nothing but the truth. They must be encouraged in this effort and helped to realize that truth-telling ultimately results in God's blessing and healing. The truth does set us free—even though truth-telling is painful.

Truth and honesty foster a rebuilding of trust. The process of truth-telling for Earl began with his confession of adultery and was followed by confession of other sins. He confessed to God, and then to me, to the Spiritual Care Team and to the children. Later he confessed to friends and colleagues, to the elders at our church, the entire congregation, clients, past and present students. Eventually he confessed to prospective employers. It seemed like telling the truth would never end. But that was good. It was lying that needed to end, not honesty. My trust level in Earl's developing character was bolstered as I witnessed Earl's return to truth and saw a willingness on his part to look me—and God—in the eye. Each time he would voluntarily share information or expand his answers to include more detail, I would gain confidence. I was encouraged as I saw his defensiveness turn toward openness.

Change is a crucial ingredient for marital restoration. Earl needed to do some things differently, not just with regard to his deceitful and sinful behavior but also in his relationship with me. This meant that he had to do some changing in areas of communication, consideration, sensitivity and understanding between us. Marital restoration is dependent on change in these crucial areas. As I began to see Earl move toward daring to change, my level of hope began to grow, ever so slowly, ever so cautiously. As he saw my belief in him growing, Earl's newfound honesty and efforts to change were reinforced. Becoming able to trust Earl again did not mean that I never raised questions or voiced concerns—such a view mitigates against true restoration. I asked plenty of questions and raised many concerns. It was important to me that Earl validate my feelings and acknowledge me as an equal person. As he responded to me openly and nondefensively, the early stages of healing began.

Honesty and change are progressive—they don't happen all at once. Each time Dr. McIvor or a team member or I would point out to Earl an area of dishonesty or need for change, his repentance would be challenged. Was he really willing to leave the old ways and go in a new direction? He had to come to believe that these confrontations were loving and not spiteful or intended to hurt. That enabled him to hear and learn rather than become defensive and walk out.

Believers need to dispel from their minds the myth that if you have forgiven someone and you love that person, you will never bring up the past. In reality, the past is inextricably woven into the present and impacts the future.

Tangible Signs

Another key element in marital restoration involves tangible expressions of change. I asked Earl for something that I felt I needed to help restore my trust and love. I requested that he give me one small thing each day that would visually remind me of his new commitment. Words have little meaning following years of lies and deceit; I needed something more. These daily, tangible expressions of love became known as "love gifts." Earl's love gift for me could be a note, a card, a flower, a small present, some service like working on my car, cooking dinner, or even a minidate like going out for a latte. My only request was that it be daily—a daily demonstration of love to me as a person and as his wife.

This process of learning to show love to me tangibly and on a daily basis was difficult for Earl. When he failed, early on, Dr. McIvor and the team forcefully challenged him to evaluate the sincerity and importance of his commitment to fulfilling my request. Carrying out the process allowed him to learn new disciplines and helped me to develop a new sense of security and to once again believe in his love. Recently the daily request has been changed to a minimum of providing a love gift on those days when he is to be gone from home. This has become a new tradition which we both enjoy.

I stayed in the relationship at the beginning because I felt God asked me to. Eventually I made a renewed commitment to the relationship because I saw Earl changing. Hope grew, but the feeling of love lagged behind. Eventually it did return, but it was slow in coming. About three years into the restoration process, I was talking with a good friend. I vividly remember the shock I felt when she said, "If I didn't know better, I'd think you were falling back in love with Earl!" Later I realized that she was right, and it felt good.

Long-term nurturing of the marriage is a must. Continuing to work together to foster love and growth in the relationship is a vital part of marital restoration. The Spiritual Care Team helped; month after month they challenged us to keep working on our issues and not to become weary.

When we grow complacent, relapse can occur. Even after the formal restoration process concluded (it was three years in length), the team was not hesitant to inquire about our continued growth. Earl reports that when he and Larry get together now, Larry asks not only how Earl is doing but how our marriage is going. Sometimes the questions are general. Other times they are quite specific: "Are you praying together? Is your sex life satisfactory? Are you spending enough time together? Are there any conflicts you are having trouble working through? What should we be praying for on your behalf?"

It is also helpful when the team points out areas of progress they are observing. This serves as an encouragement to the restoree and spouse, who may not have taken time to notice any progress. It was exciting to Earl and me when others began to notice that our level of affection for each other seemed to be deepening.

Reaching Out to the Children
Our children, whose ages in 1989 ranged from fifteen to twenty-

five, were devastated and confused when they learned of the double life their father had been living. Each of the five was deeply wounded. But their responses to Earl's infidelities varied according to the age and temperament of each child. At various times they experienced anger, fear, withdrawal, abandonment and denial.

Their idea of the perfect family didn't fit us anymore. They were embarrassed to tell their friends and yet needed someone to talk with. They were afraid that Earl and I might divorce; they were scared that AIDS might enter the picture. Acutely feeling the loss of old certainties, they weren't sure how they felt about their dad. Some didn't want to think about their feelings; others needed to ponder things before they could talk.

From the beginning the Spiritual Care Team—particularly Paul and Virginia, who knew our family best—tried to make themselves available to our kids. Their efforts were sometimes rebuffed. While Earl and I wanted Paul and Virginia to act as the children's "advocates," or at least their confidants, it didn't work completely. One of our daughters said, "We don't like to get together with Paul and Virginia. We're afraid we'll hear more things that we don't want to hear." There is still need for a lot of healing in our family, even seven years later.

What about other situations where children's lives have been deeply affected by the intrusive power of a parent's sin? What if the children had been younger? What if no one had stepped up to help their parents? What if no one had tried to reach out to them? What if there had been a divorce?

We are aware of a number of family situations where there did not seem to be repentance and the result was a broken marriage. The consequences can be devastating for the children. Consider, for example, the impact of changing homes and starting in new schools. What happens to friendships, economic status and social position at church and school? Increased anxiety, uncertainty, fear, confusion, anger and overwhelming personal loss will dominate the life of a child, adolescent or young adult.

In one example that came to our attention, a pastor and father of three young girls had an affair with one of the girls' married Sunday-school teachers. When disclosure came, it was a complete surprise to the girls. Their father seemed repentant, or at least sorry for the disgrace he had brought on them. He subsequently lost his job, then had another affair. Eventually he and his wife divorced. The girls felt they had no one to turn to. As a result they turned away from their parents—and from God. They found solace as they grew older in complete rebellion against religious matters. They were convinced that their father never had repented and was sorry only that he got caught.

These girls' lives were thrown into total and long-lasting upheaval. Things might have been different for them if their father had been truly repentant and committed to change. Things might have been better if they had at least had an advocate or friend in whom they could confide. Lacking both, they turned inward and rebelled.

It was eight years before two of the girls were brought by a friend to work at a Christian summer camp. This friend had known them for over a decade—and had seen them go from being happy children in a widely respected Christian family to being rebellious, wounded, self-destructive victims of a broken home and an abandoning father. Having confidence that the girls would be open to change in an environment of safety and love, this dear friend brought them to the camp. And the camp became for them a place of healing and truth where, by God's grace, they reconnected with their loving, forgiving heavenly Father. But for the grace of God they might have been lost completely.

It is very difficult for a Spiritual Care Team to anticipate the needs of the children in a given situation. So much depends on their ages and individual personalities.

Preschool children want to understand what has happened but may not be prepared for what they learn. They will need patient support. Those who try to minister to them must realize that they will be very aware of conflicts between their parents. The disruptions that occur during separation, divorce or other family-threatening events are devastating.

The Spiritual Care Team may help by assessing the positive relationships in the family and encouraging other significant family members—grandparents, aunts and uncles, older siblings—to get involved. Time spent with the children, giving affirmation and doing lots of listening, can lend stability to their disturbed lives. These family support people may also assist the parents by providing tangible assistance, such as child care, so the parents will have more uninterrupted time to work through their conflicts.

Preteen children often believe that they have somehow caused the problem. Most will experience personal rejection and will feel guilty. They need strong, caring adults to be around them, offering affirmation (and assuring them that what happened was *not* their fault), and they also need their parents' continued attention and affection. They should be told the truth and allowed to ask questions. Telling them they are too young to understand only creates more confusion and anger.

Teenagers whose families have been disrupted have very great needs. Their lives have been turned upside down at a time when they most need stability. Teens are naturally concerned about what people will think, and they'll be convinced that others think the worst possible things about them now. Deep inside they will have questions about God, sex, marriage, parental love and various personal matters—but they may only express superficialities. The Spiritual Care Team should not be alarmed to hear that the first question a teen may have is "Does this mean I don't get to buy a car?" Teens are very aware that the behavior of parents has a strong impact on their egocentric lives.

Most teens choose to confide in their friends, who are usually not mature enough to provide guidance. It is important to encourage them to seek out adult friends to whom they feel comfortable talking about the upheaval they are in. (Let them pick one or two if possible.) Teachers, youth leaders, coaches, neighbors and relatives can be helpful. Spiritual Care Team members should be available and supportive but will have to earn the right to be heard. Group counseling is the best form of intervention. School counselors and local mental-health organizations can be good resources for finding appropriate groups.

Adult children are not immune to the pain. When considering the needs of the restoree's children, do not overlook those who are married or gone from the home. Their depth of hurt and confusion will not be any less than that of the younger children. They need to talk; they need to know what's going on, and they need to be able to voice their opinions. We recommend that the Spiritual Care Team contact each son or daughter and let him or her know about the goals and activities of the team regarding the parent's restoration. When possible, meet with them personally; encourage the restoree to communicate with the adult children about the spiritual journey that is part of the restoration process.

How Much to Tell

How much disclosure is helpful and necessary for the child of a fallen adult? Honesty is again the key. Children need the truth, though the amount of detail shared should be age-appropriate.

Sue's parents divorced when she was twelve years old. Sue was told it was because they just didn't get along. When she was twenty-nine, her aunt let it slip that the reason for the divorce had been Sue's mother's unfaithfulness. Though shocked by the news of the affair, Sue was devastated primarily by her parents' dishonesty with her.

With a child of any age, the overarching principle regarding disclosure is honesty. A child should never be left vulnerable to hearing "the real truth" from someone else. If a child is old enough to be given misleading information, he or she is old enough to receive accurate information from you. The amount of detail will be determined by the understanding level of the child. But there should be a commitment to answering any question posed by the child unless it is inappropriate ("What did you do in the massage parlor, Dad?"). An acceptable response to an inappropriate question is, "I don't feel that information is appropriate or helpful for you." (Be careful not to use this response as a cop-out from answering valid questions.)

Family Tips

Here are seven key areas that were particularly important as the children and I worked through our responses to Earl's unfaithfulness.

1. Time, time and more time is required for the spouse and children to process the pain the restoree's sin has foisted upon them. Remember that the responsible party has most likely been immersed in the sinful behavior for a long time, possibly years. This person may be pressing for a quick return to normalcy while the spouse and children are still reeling from the shock. The restoree must be patient while the wounded family members work through their pain.

2. The period immediately after disclosure is a roller coaster of emotion for everyone. The spouse in particular goes through devastating feelings of betrayal, rejection and anger. The children go through terrible feelings of abandonment, fear and uncertainty. Everyone must be given an opportunity to work through the problem at their own pace and in their own way. Don't expect that the process will proceed according to any set pattern; be sensitive to individual needs.

3. Both the spouse and the children need outside support. In my case, sometimes what I needed was just someone to hold me or sit quietly and let me talk. I am convinced that children need this kind of support as well. Too often, because children do not understand or have more difficulty verbalizing their fears, we adults do not recognize or acknowledge their needs. Studies indicate that the delayed response of some children to a divorce happens because parents or counselors fail to deal with their insecurities early on. The children need someone to come alongside them quickly—someone they can trust and talk to when they become willing to do so.

4. An underlying, all-important issue is honesty. Both the spouse and the children need to know the truth about what they are facing. The offender also needs to face the truth and must not be allowed to gloss over or deny reality. Honesty allows for clarification of responsibility for the sin and for appropriate planning of healthy next steps. Resist the temptation to reduce the pain for people by allowing less than total honesty.

5. The spouse needs support (in an appropriate fashion) from the opposite sex. At a time when my self-esteem was terribly fragile, the men on the Spiritual Care Team were extremely helpful in affirming and encouraging me as a valid person. And it was very reassuring to me to see them providing "tough-love" accountability for Earl.

6. Appropriate professional counseling is also important, not only for the party involved in the sin but also for the spouse and children. The input of an independent, objective observer who has dealt with many situations similar to this one can help promote the healing process.

7. If a divorce occurs because reconciliation is not accomplished, do not neglect or forget the victims. Too often the spouse and children become isolated and left out. The young daughters of the pastor in the earlier story felt completely rejected by the

church. Their bitterness then turned to sin, arising out of their feelings of abandonment by their church as well as by their father. Their eight years of wandering in sinfulness might have been avoided if a Spiritual Care Team had been created to stand in the gap.

How the Team Helped

The Spiritual Care Team that helped our family offered us four main things—things that made a tremendous difference as we faced the biggest trauma of our lives.

1. The Spiritual Care Team provided *security* for the children and me. Our family always knew there was someone we could call who would pray for us. Even when we didn't take advantage of the opportunity to call on the team, we had a sense of security; we all knew there were people available to provide encouragement and support.

2. The Spiritual Care Team offered *stability* to all the family members during a time of great disruption. When someone would panic, a team member would listen and reply with calmness. When anger raged, there was someone to hear and provide understanding. The team was able to help us to remain stable during the times of greatest tumult. The children's concerns were lightened as they saw the calming effect the team had on me. And it was good for them to know that someone was helping their dad get his life stabilized.

3. The Spiritual Care Team gave *support* to the family. Team members stood against wrong; they cared enough about us to challenge us when we wandered into wrong attitudes or words. They walked alongside as various family members tried to follow God's lead in the healing process. They often urged me on when I needed to stand up to Earl, and they helped me believe it was worth hanging on when I was finding it hard to stay in the marriage. The team also helped by offering explanation and

encouragement to the children when hurt and confusion would well up.

4. Finally, the Spiritual Care Team provided a real *spiritual challenge* to our family. Some of us wondered, *Where is God in all this?* The team reminded us, "We dare not lose sight of what God is wanting to accomplish through this mess. He desires to bring the whole family back to himself." The team faithfully reminded us that God's love and mercy are greater than all sin—that God's desire is to work inside each person to bring healing and restoration. At such a spiritually vulnerable time, their faith, hope and love meant a tremendous amount to us. I don't know where we would be now if this team had not encircled us and been God's instrument for healing in these ways.

10

The Role of Professional Helpers

The role of Christian counseling and psychology in the church is widely debated and is the subject of ongoing controversy. The issue is even more controversial in situations where the problem areas are clearly matters of sin. Is a professional helper necessary? Does the offender just need to be told to get right with God and get on with life? Some people fear that involving counselors or psychologists will only provide the offender with a rationalization for their wrong behavior and thus hinder them from actually dealing with sin. Pastors who must deal with very complicated patterns of sin and deceit may be overwhelmed and decide to place the responsibility for helping the offender in the hands of someone they see as better trained. Is this wise, or is it simply avoiding a God-given responsibility? Does it have to be one or the other?

When Sandy first insisted that I get professional help, my

reaction was to resist. I was still denying or minimizing what I had done, and a part of that denial was to reject the need for professional help. "I don't need counseling. After all, I'm a psychologist. I can figure this thing out." I said this at a time when my level of fear and confusion was so high that I could hardly remember how to write my name or where I had parked my car! I was also unaware, at that point, of just how much the "I can take care of things on my own" attitude was a part of my sinful, self-defeating behavior. I was protecting myself, trying to maintain secrecy, trying to prop up my self-esteem by telling myself, *At least you don't need therapy.* I was still living the lie, not willing to submit to authority—the authority of God or of a human expert.

Sandy wisely held her ground. She knew me, and she knew how reluctant I was to ask for help even when I needed it. We laugh now when we think about my saying, "Well, maybe I'll just go once, to make sure I'm on the right track." We talked about possibilities and discussed professionals we knew either personally or by reputation. No clear candidate surfaced. We talked about finding someone who was strong enough to see through my self-justification and my ability to present myself in the most positive light. I don't recall ever praying about the matter—I don't usually pray about things I don't want. Sandy must have been praying, however, and God was at work. One day as I was thinking that I needed to see someone just to satisfy Sandy, if for no other reason, the name of Dr. Daniel McIvor came to mind. I remembered taking a couple of continuing education classes from him and had been impressed with him both personally and professionally. I also remembered his talking about people *lying by omission.* And down deep I knew that lying and deceit had as much to do with my problem as the sexual sin.

I decided to see him. I told Sandy about my decision and called for an appointment. I was afraid—very afraid. His voice was warm and friendly over the telephone, and we set a date for the first meeting. I felt relieved that he couldn't see me for a couple of weeks. I'm sure I was thinking that maybe everything would get resolved before then and I wouldn't need to go. The denial was still very strong; I was still very closed.

I told Sandy that because of the distance I had to go and because of my poor memory, I was going to get a good tape recorder and tape the sessions. *I might as well get my money's worth,* I thought. Soon I was on my way. Seeing the therapist was one more thing I could check off my list. It was right below seeing my attorney. Just one more detail to take care of.

Dr. McIvor was cordial but not overly friendly. He certainly didn't say anything to make me feel better. I remember thinking that I had liked him better as a teacher. When I mentioned recording the sessions, he surprised me by saying, "No. Maybe later on—but I want to consult with a colleague before I decide about that." So far things weren't really going my way.

And it got worse fast. I showed him the letter I had received from the Board of Psychologist Examiners and the response I had sent. I wasn't ready for his reaction. He glanced up from the letters, looked me right in the eye and said, "If I was on the board, I'd pull your license immediately."

"Why?" I said, almost in shock.

His reply hit hard. "Because you are totally denying any responsibility for what you did."

I said, "No, I'm not. That's just the way the attorney wrote the letter."

He said curtly, "I don't see his name here; I only see yours. You're responsible for anything and everything that goes out over your signature."

I was sobered. I felt out of control. I was also more afraid than ever, because I had already sent the letter.

The next issue was truth-telling. "I'll have no way to know

whether you're lying or withholding information from me," he said, "unless you allow me to talk to Sandy and other people who are close to you. Will you be willing to sign the necessary release of information so that I can talk to those people?"

I agreed, but I remember thinking, *Hey, I'm not used to having people question my honesty.* I prided myself in believing that I was an honest, trustworthy person. The level of my self-deceit was that high!

But I stayed, and by the time the session was over Dr. McIvor had helped me to begin to articulate six long-term goals:

☐ To be a man of integrity.

☐ To be sexually pure.

☐ To tell the truth.

☐ To be ethical in all aspects of my professional practice.

☐ To rebuild my marriage with Sandy.

☐ To rebuild my relationship with the children.

I left the office that day in a state of shock. I could see so many areas in which I needed help. I was dazed and amazed. I had even made an appointment to come back—the next time for a double session.

I called Sandy from a pay phone to tell her I was starting the drive home. A surge of emotion caused my voice to crack as I told her I had found the right person. "He's tough enough," I said. For the first time I was admitting to myself the depth of my need. I began to cry as this admission turned to hope.

During the weeks, months and years of my restoration process, Dr. McIvor has been very important to me—and to Sandy, the restoration team and, less directly, the children. His clear-cut understanding of the problem was a source of guidance and encouragement for the team. Several characteristics that he exhibited may serve as guidelines for selecting a therapist in general and for finding a therapist who can work as part of a restoration process. Be sure you find a counselor who has:

☐ a clear understanding of your problem

☐ experience in directing treatment for your specific type of problem

☐ a willingness to work cooperatively with other resource people, such as your Spiritual Care Team

☐ an understanding of Christian values and a willingness to work within the value system that you and the restoration team share

☐ the ability to confront while maintaining a good working relationship

Understanding the Problem

In our experience many pastoral counselors and Christian psychologists are reluctant to be forceful and confrontative with clients. Unfortunately, there seems to be an unwritten rule that if you believe in forgiveness and God's cleansing for a person, then you should not be tough or confrontative. This is a dangerous approach, particularly in those instances where patterns of sin and deceit have existed for a long time. The perception of the problem by people in need of restoration is usually so distorted that they may never truly come to grips with the issues without a conscious effort on the part of the therapist to make them uncomfortable. Look at some of the common rationalizations:

☐ "Joe has fallen into sin." Wrong! Joe has deliberately made sinful choices for a long period of time.

☐ "Joe couldn't help himself—the urge was just too strong." No! Joe has resisted help that was offered and has kept secret his sinful behavior pattern.

☐ "I don't think Joe really intended to hurt anybody." So! Does that change the fact that grave damage has been done and many people have been hurt deeply?

To thoroughly understand the problem requires an awareness of more than just the psychological mechanisms involved. If full restoration is to take place, the entire impact must be considered and each aspect of the situation thoroughly probed. The offender must be helped to realize the extent of the hurt he or she has brought to others so that authentic forgiveness can be asked for and granted. Our families and churches are full of walking wounded who have been told that they should be satisfied with a muffled statement of "I'm sorry" from an offender who may have no idea of the extent of the damage he or she is "apologizing" for.

A good therapist can help the offender to consider all aspects of the problem, including the impact of the offender's behavior on others. One person said, "I had justified what I was doing by telling myself that I wasn't really hurting anyone. When I learned just how wrong I was, I knew I had to stop."

Select a therapist who understands your specific problem. The role of the therapist is to be a careful observer and to help restorees squarely face their issues. The more the therapist understands the problem, the greater the likelihood that a restoree will be helped to face his or her issues in ways that will lead to positive outcomes. A therapist, Christian or non-Christian, will not be helpful unless he or she has enough awareness of the problem to help the restoree face the key issues.

There's No Substitute for Experience

A therapist who has never counseled a shoplifter or compulsive gambler may know very little about the dynamics of this type of problem. How can this therapist help lead the person to a solution? Do not hesitate to ask any professional, including your pastor, about his or her experience in dealing with a specific problem. They have an ethical and moral obligation not to provide services in areas where they have not had experience or training. If the experience or training is inadequate, the pastor or counselor may still be helpful, but the areas of help should be clearly specified and the areas of responsibility delineated. Where experience or training are insufficient, the professional may still work with the person but should not do so without seeking help from another professional with the necessary training and experience.

Dr. McIvor was trained and experienced enough to work with me, but he still chose to get consultation from someone even more experienced to ensure that I got the highest level of care. The Spiritual Care Team members, who had very limited experience in leading people through the restoration process, also consulted others, including Dr. McIvor and several people who had been involved in guiding restoration efforts. Never hesitate to ask about experience, and always be willing to get further input when your own understanding is limited.

Therapist and Team

In the fall of 1991, two years after this process began, the team met at the Friesens' home. Initially we had thought the restoration process might take about two years. Earl anticipated receiving permission, at its completion, to return to his ministry activities. In October 1991, he received the official decision of the Oregon Board of Psychologist Examiners, putting him on probation and requiring that he not do any counseling work for one year. (The probation arose out of the complaint from his former client with whom he had had the affair.)

Paul was the person to whom the team had delegated responsibility for communicating with my therapist. He recalls a day soon after our October meeting:

I shall never forget the knot in my stomach as I walked into our apartment and Virginia handed me the phone with a wry smile, saying, "It's Dr. McIvor."

I had spoken with Dr. McIvor several times in the past two years but was uneasy about this unexpected call. The Spiritual Care Team had met the previous weekend and concluded that it would be premature for Earl to resume his writing and speaking. With the awareness that his suspended license would preclude his work as a therapist, we saw the potential for Earl to learn to be alone with God. We sensed that significant internal work still needed to be done, and we feared that the potential growth would be swallowed up by a shift in his focus.

Earl had come to the meeting with the eager expectation of release. He was devastated—and angry—at our directive. I assumed that this call from Dr. McIvor was about our decision. I wasn't sure exactly what this therapist thought of our team's involvement in Earl's life—and I was worried that he was about to make it very clear what he thought of us!

I was afraid he would say we had made a mistake in telling Earl not to seek work. Would he see our decision as counterproductive to his efforts to return Earl to a healthy lifestyle? His first statement was, "So I understand you told Earl you didn't feel he was ready to resume speaking and writing, and you even discouraged him from finding work this coming year."

I gulped and said, "Yes, that's true."

He then asked how we had arrived at that conclusion. What I heard was, "How did *you* (meaning just me) arrive at such a conclusion?" I gulped again, offered a quick prayer and said with all the confidence I could muster that *we* (plural) had felt that some of the issues at the root of Earl's problems were still there, such as his self-sufficiency, earning worth by activity, finding status by speaking and writing, self-centeredness rather than God-centeredness and so on. I said we were also concerned that he hadn't yet dealt with issues related to his children.

I finished talking and expected his response to be the doctoral equivalent of "You idiot!" Instead I heard, "I couldn't agree with you more, and I just wanted to affirm your direction with Earl." I began to breathe again.

Without communication with the therapist, the team cannot know what kind of input the restoree is receiving or whether or not the two efforts are compatible. Both efforts are necessary; the importance of good communication and cooperation cannot be overemphasized.

Willingness to Work with Christian Values

Life for the restoree is confusing enough without having to deal with the confusion of conflicting advice from various sources. Where conflicts exist, address them up front with the restoree so that he or she does not feel caught in the middle.

Our experience working with Dr. Daniel McIvor was wonderful. I respected his professional advice and thus would work on issues he raised. I also respected the team's desire to see me through this whole experience and care for me spiritually. Although Dr. McIvor did not view the life of faith in the same way we did, he shared the values the team was trying to encourage. Not only was he sympathetic with our positions of faith, but also, more than once, he challenged us on beliefs to which we gave lip service but which we may not have been practicing.

What does the Spiritual Care Team do when the advice of the therapist conflicts with their own advice? Some would say that a Christian should seek out only a Christian therapist, but what does this really mean? There is great diversity even among Christian therapists. Unfortunately, some Christian therapists might advise "covering up" or other actions that are the opposite of sound biblical principles of restoration. Careful evaluation of the beliefs and style of the prospective therapist is essential. Ask, "Who is the most qualified therapist in this specific area that has a value system compatible with the Christian view?" If I were having surgery, I would be delighted if my doctor were a Christian, but I'd be more interested in the doctor's skill as a surgeon.

The Ability to Confront

Restoration implies that a failure has occurred. If a person has not fallen, he or she does not need to be restored. Recognizing this does not mean that the restoree is immediately able to deal with the failure or to consider all that may be needed in order to complete the restoration process. A good therapist will be able to gradually confront the restoree with pertinent issues for consideration while maintaining an atmosphere of trust.

There were many times when I did not like what Dr. McIvor had to say. It is difficult to admit past failure, and it was even more difficult for me to focus on my current weaknesses and shortcomings. But I soon came to trust Dr. McIvor and believe that he had my best interest at heart, even when his words were hard to hear.

Sandy remembers, "I couldn't believe my ears. Dr. McIvor told Earl that I was the most rational one in our family right now and that he needed to listen to me if he wanted to avoid some serious mistakes. No one had ever talked to Earl that way before!"

Dr. McIvor refused to take the easy way out. He was thorough and persistent, unwilling to let me gloss over weaknesses and avoid the pain that the call to restoration demands. He refused to be manipulated into thinking that I could get on with my life without addressing weakness and character flaws and admitting the need for change. His genuine caring came through and sustained the growth process.

We began this chapter by asking, Is a professional counselor a necessary part of the restoration process? Yes. Having the "right" counselor is a tremendous help in facilitating the healing process.

One caution: the spiritual care team cannot be all things to all people. When in-depth counseling or therapy is needed, it should be provided by someone other than team members. We also believe that the restoree's pastor should not be the therapist. His role is to pastor the person and the family. When everyone works together, God brings healing.

11

The Church's Role in Restoration

*M**any churches are* unprepared to deal with sinful and destructive behavior patterns in their members. Yet it is important that a person undergoing the restoration process receive help from his or her church—in the form of the ministries of discipline and love.

When the events in my life came to light, our family's church—a large and sophisticated one—had great difficulty accepting and dealing with the situation. This was complicated by the absence of a senior pastor at the time. As a result, I did not go immediately to the church for help. Instead, I asked Larry, Nancy, Paul and Virginia to form a Spiritual Care Team to give me spiritual guidance, and I talked with a few other close friends as well. But eventually, Sandy and I agreed with the team that it was necessary to go to the church. It was uncomfortable for us to be in the church when people there didn't know the full truth. And philosophically, we all believed that there was a joint responsibility between the church and the restoree to work together in matters of restoration.

Finally a new senior pastor arrived. As our first step in dealing with the church, Sandy and I went to him so I could confess my sin and we could explain our situation. He was concerned and empathetic, yet careful in his attempts to evaluate the status of repentance and my current level of spiritual vitality. On one occasion he met with the Spiritual Care Team to discuss their role and how he could be of assistance to the team and to us. The pastor then reported to the church board of elders, who appeared reluctant to get involved and seemed to support a keep-it-quiet point of view.

The second step in disclosure with regard to the church was for Sandy and me to go before the board of elders. There I again confessed my sin. I had already talked privately with certain past and present church leaders with whom I had once shared church leadership responsibilities. The board and other church leaders were sympathetic. Somewhat uncertain of how to proceed, they decided to "work it out" privately. In fact, several people appeared threatened by the disclosures and did not want to get involved. They seemed pleased that there was a Spiritual Care Team that they could rely on. Since Sandy and I were still attending the church, it seemed logical to the six of us on the team that the local church should be involved more closely in the restoration process.

Sandy and I asked for a representative couple from the church (preferably from the board of elders) to join the Spiritual Care Team, and the elders appointed one. The husband met with the team briefly on one occasion. But the couple did not become involved in the Spiritual Care Team, so the attempt at unification of the team and the local church failed. Perhaps better results might have been attained if the unification could have been attempted earlier. It is difficult for a couple to be added when a process is well under way.

The church leadership remained distant. Individual church members who knew about my situation responded in various ways. Most were confused by not having heard the truth from me and didn't know how to respond. For the most part, the issues were ignored. All in all it was a very uncomfortable situation.

When the elder board discouraged a public confession, attending church became more and more difficult. It seemed as if those who knew the truth were committed to keeping the situation secret, while those who didn't know asked questions that made it hard to keep the silence the elders seemed to prefer. Sandy grew tired of having to answer questions like "How's that wonderful husband of yours?" She refused to lie, but felt restrained from sharing the truth. Feeling lonely, angry and unsupported by her church, she no longer wanted to be there.

With the encouragement of the team, we met again with the pastor and his wife and shared our dilemma with them. Sandy did not feel she could continue attending unless the truth was made public. I agreed, although I was terrified at the thought of additional exposure. The pastor listened and understood. He said he would pray about the situation, and he arranged a time for a public confession.

That occasion paved the way for Sandy and me to be able to reinvolve ourselves in an appropriate way with the local church body. We no longer had to hide or be concerned with who knew what. It was surprisingly liberating to be publicly released from my years of hiding and secret-keeping. We now felt free to attend regularly, to get involved in a small group where we could be accepted and cared for—and I felt free to begin attending the morning men's Bible study, where I could be ministered to by the pastor and the other men who came.

What's the Right Approach?

In earlier chapters we discussed how the church seems to respond to major sin in one of its members in one of three ways. The first may be termed "cheap grace"—a quick, nonconfronting, short-term approach to the problem: accept the individual's apology and let it go at that. Some short-term effort may be extended to assist the individual, but the spouse and kids usually get only lip service. Efforts are shallow and woefully inadequate.

The second approach is the legalistic response, which may result in actual banishment of the sinner from the church. Some churches call this excommunication. This is also a short-term, quick-fix process wherein the individual is publicly or privately asked or told to leave the church. Little thought is given to restoration of the individual to fellowship with God or with the church family. And the recovery of the spouse and family members is ignored.

The third and probably most frequent response is to ignore the problem altogether. The church leaders may suggest counseling; the pastor may even counsel the individual or individuals on a short-term basis. But nothing is made public, and the process does not involve accountability or follow-up. The injured family lives among rumors and has to find its own way to healing.

Steve, a pastor friend of mine, began keeping track of fallen leaders whom he knew personally or who had made an impact on his life. His list now contains over twenty names. He found that only one of them had gone through a formal restoration process that met his needs and those of the church family. "Offenders just left the church," Steve stated. "Often they took a short time out and then went back to ministry. No one was there to aid them in the restoration process or even to verify that restoration had taken place. Other offenders just left the ministry without any follow-up."

A Better Way

We suggest a fourth alternative. It is neither short-term nor easy. It involves accountability, commitment to all members of the family and quite often a public disclosure. The church should take the lead in this process. In my case the church was not prepared to deal with the situation. However, in a subsequent situation that arose within this same church, the people were able to deal with the situation more purposefully and effectively. This may have been due in part to what they had learned from my situation.

Sandy and I participated in the restoration process of a young pastor from our church. We became members of his Spiritual Care Team, and this involvement set in motion a learning process for the entire church. Seven other people who were members of this Spiritual Care Team were able to learn from our mentoring, for we passed along what had been helpful to us.

Through our own experience with our local church and through what we've seen in other churches, we are convinced that, ideally, all restoration should be closely tied to the local church of the fallen believer.

In studying Scripture we notice that teaching on discipline and restoration is always tied to a local fellowship and not simply to a group of well-intentioned friends. Our theme verses, Galatians 6:1-2, speak of brothers (plural) restoring an individual. The admonition to carry each other's burdens was given to the churches in Galatia. We are also instructed to confess our sins to each other (Jas 5:13-16). The confession, read in context, is to take place within the fellowship of believers. The sick person is to call on the elders. Thus the process of confession and healing is to be carried out not as lone rangers but as fellow members of the local assembly of the family of God.

The process of disciplining a fellow believer is spelled out in Matthew 18:15-17. If the offender is not receptive to the person or persons who confront him, the confronting person is to "tell it to the church." Centuries earlier, God sent the prophet Nathan to confront King David about his sin against the Lord: adultery, murder and deception. After Nathan's courageous truth-telling, David repented, and then he "went into the house of the LORD and worshiped" (2 Sam 12:20). It is clear that God wants to surround the fallen believer with brothers and sisters in the church who are able to exercise discipline and to gently restore.

Nine Traits of a Restoring Church

But not all churches meet the ideal. What kind of place does a church need to be in order to be used by God as a restoring church? Here are nine important traits.

A restoring church is

1. A safe place for people to be real. In too many churches it is anything but safe to be authentic about our life situations. It has been said that more lying is done on Sunday morning than at any other time in the week. Individuals and families work very hard at not admitting their faults, sins and shortcomings. Why? They fear rejection.

Teaching a Sunday-school class, Paul Friesen illustrated a point by telling about the time he was stopped for speeding. After class a man came up and thanked him for his helpful teaching. Paul waited to hear what theological insight the man had received—but the man simply added, "I liked you telling about getting stopped by the policeman. I never heard a pastor admit something like that before." Folks think, *I haven't seen leaders be real in church, so I'd better not be real either.*

In one church we know of, a climate of authenticity has begun to be established. Recently a man got up in a prayer meeting and asked for prayer for his addiction to pornography. This church is beginning to be a safe place for confession; it will likely become a safe place for restoration.

Becky Pippert, reflecting on Christians not feeling safe enough to be real, tells of auditing a course at Harvard University:

The students were extraordinarily open and candid about their problems. It wasn't uncommon to hear them say, "I'm angry," "I'm afraid," "I'm jealous." . . . One day after class, I dropped in on a Bible study group in Cambridge. It would be unfair to overdraw the contrast, but it was striking. No one spoke openly about his or her problems. . . . This kind of suppression of unpleasantness is common in certain religious circles in America, where the expectation is that we must smile, be upbeat and always victorious. One reason for this is that, in the stress of our modern society, we are insecure and afraid. Afraid that if we share who we are or what we are really feeling, we might lose our standing in the eyes of others, or God, or ourselves. If we expose our weakness, everyone will see we are not as mature in faith as was thought. (*Hope Has Its Reasons* [New York: Harper & Row, 1989], pp. 20-21)

2. A place where godly judgment is administered. In 1 Corinthians 5:12-13, the apostle Paul tells the church, "Are you not to judge those inside [the church]? God will judge those outside. 'Expel the wicked man from among you.' " Being a safe place should not imply that the church is not sensitive to sin and committed to dealing with it. Internal conviction often brings us to repentance, but sometimes it takes a loving brother or sister who has observed us and is willing to challenge us to do something about it. A church that looks the other way and does not confront sin in its midst will not be a restoring church.

At the same time, it needs to be clear that confronting sin does not mean blasting sinners; the confrontation should always be done gently (Gal 6:1).

3. A place where grace is extended. A place where sin is confronted is not therefore a place void of grace. When Jesus extended grace to the woman taken in adultery, he did not ignore her sin: "Neither do I condemn you. . . . Go now and leave your life of sin" (Jn 8:11). A grace-giving church lets people know this is a place where repentant sinners are able to "approach the throne of grace with confidence, so that we may receive mercy and find grace to help us in our time of need" (Heb 4:16). The only time you can approach with confidence someone you have wronged is when you know that this is a person committed to extending mercy and grace. God is like this; his church body should be like this as well.

4. A place for discipline. Hebrews 12:1-13 speaks of the loving discipline of our heavenly Father. It tells us honestly that "no discipline seems pleasant at the time" (v. 11), but it goes on to say that it produces, for those who have been trained by it, "a harvest of righteousness and peace." A restoring church is not afraid to enter into loving but firm church discipline where necessary. Some individuals are not willing to participate in the restoration process. Where there is no repentance, the church is instructed to extend discipline.

I am aware of a church in which an elder was living a life of sin. He was confronted by one individual, then by that person along with witnesses, and finally by all the elders. Nothing happened. Finally the pastor stood up one Sunday and sadly explained that this man had been admonished, according to the process prescribed in Matthew 18, but had refused to change his ways, so he should be regarded as a pagan until he repented of his sin. Such statements should not be entered into quickly or lightly, but, for the integrity of the body of Christ, they must be made if the person refuses to repent. We are told to "expel the wicked" (1 Cor 5:13), not to quietly tolerate them.

5. A place for accountability. Those holding us accountable need to be people who know us well. Brothers and sisters in our church can do it better than a friend living far away, simply because they see us regularly. We need to give them permission to ask us the hard questions.

It is often helpful to actually give a list of questions to each of the people who agree to hold us accountable. They can ask any of these questions anytime we are together. Writing the questions ourselves is wise because we likely know our own areas of weakness better than an outside observer. Five questions to be used in my own situation might be these:

1. Have you read, seen or listened to anything this last week that was sexually inappropriate?

2. Have you withheld information from others in order to put yourself in a more positive light?

3. What have you done this week to express your love to Sandy?

4. What have your patterns been in the area of spiritual disciplines?

5. Have you been less than truthful in any of your answers?

Many of us want to be good, but not *that* good! We want to cut down on a sinful habit, but we don't want to eliminate it altogether. Accountability groups or relationships help us to move toward a more authentic, God-pleasing lifestyle.

Another very important reason to be part of an accountability group in your church is that confession to a brother or sister is able to bring great freedom. Dietrich Bonhoeffer explains, "Since the confession of sin is made in the presence of a Christian brother, the last stronghold of self-justification is abandoned. The sinner surrenders; he gives up all his evil. He gives his heart to God, and he finds the forgiveness of all his sin in the fellowship of Jesus Christ and his brother" (*Life Together* [New York: Harper & Brothers, 1954], p. 112).

6. A place where truth-telling is practiced. Ephesians 4:25 instructs us, "Each of you must put off falsehood and speak truthfully to his neighbor, for we are all members of one body." When we are untruthful, we hurt not only ourselves but the whole body of believers. Phrases such as "I'll tell you this if you promise not to tell where you heard it" and "If I told the truth it would hurt too many people" buy into the lie that honesty is not always the best policy. Announcing only that "Pastor Smith resigned for personal reasons" implies that Pastor Smith's personal life has nothing to do with the rest of us. But in the body of Christ our lives are to be open to each other, not filled with secrets. If restoration is going to happen in your church, you must be committed to truth-telling as a means of curtailing sinful patterns.

Another reason for honesty is that truth stops rumors. When information is withheld or distorted, people tend to fill in the blanks. *That was a nice resignation speech the worship leader gave about the Lord leading her to leave the church. But she doesn't know where she's going—what's the real reason she's leaving? Maybe she was fired. I'll bet the pastor was threatened by her popularity . . .* It's not appropriate to disclose every detail, of course, but the more truth told the better. Avoid putting a spin on the story that will protect a person or preserve church unity but isn't really true. If statements are circulating that aren't true, they should be addressed.

7. A place where the restoree is validated for return to ministry. When Saul the Pharisee, enemy of Christians, was converted (and became the apostle Paul), he scared the Christians in Jerusalem by showing up on their doorstep—and trying to join them! *Isn't this the man who was making murderous threats against Christians and trying to put them in prison?* But Barnabas spoke on his behalf, assuring them that Saul had met Jesus and was now one of them. Similarly, restoration sometimes requires an advocate to speak on behalf of a fallen brother or sister in whom God has brought about repentance and change.

Andy, an assistant pastor, recalls his role in being an advocate for me at church:

I had my first taste of the value of a Spiritual Care Team when our church began to consider the possibility of opening up a working relationship with Earl Wilson. Because I had made referrals to him prior to the exposure of his sin and had had several in-depth conversations with him during the period of his restoration, I ended up being the one who took the initiative during elder meetings to give shape to the process. I realized at the time that the elders had an immense burden to bear when it came to protecting the well-being and integrity of this body. Because the elders were looking to me to vouch for Earl and the effectiveness of his restoration process, I realized that our very competence as leaders was on the line.

I had a conversation with Larry Paulson, who was a member of Earl's Spiritual Care Team. Having spent intense time with the team for the last several years working through the painful process of repentance and rebuilding, Larry was able to give me the tangible evidence of restoration that I needed to be able to say with confidence that we could place our trust in Earl. I believe that Spiritual Care Teams, useful in a number of problem areas, are especially helpful for the task of rebuilding trust. When an individual's life has had covertly evil components to it, or when he or she has successfully compartmentalized beliefs and behavior to the point that those nearby are unaware of inconsistencies, then the person has forfeited the right to say—or imply—"Trust me." The only way to be restored is by submitting to the scrutiny of trustworthy individuals who at some point in the healing process can say that they are willing to vouch for the fact that the restored individual has regained his or her integrity.

There was also an occasion when I was being considered for a teaching post at a seminary and a letter of reference was required to "ensure" that I had been properly restored. The seminary appreciated the work of the Spiritual Care Team; still they insisted on a letter from my church expressing commitment to my restoration process and an evaluation of the result.

8. A place that is a haven for the fallen person's family. Too often the spouse and children of the offender are treated as if the sin was their fault. Some members of the church may perhaps stop talking with them at church and even avoid them in other public places. Perhaps these folks just don't know what to say—or perhaps they lump the family members in with the sinful behavior of the one committing the sin. Such a mistake can severely damage the faith of family members at a time when they need to be understood and loved rather than pushed away. It is extremely important for the church to stand with them in support during this traumatic time.

Pitfalls of Do-It-Yourself Restoration

George phoned Paul and Virginia to ask for assistance in dealing with an elder in his church who had been involved in an affair. When the concept of a Spiritual Care Team was explained to the elder, he was clearly not impressed. He finally said he was willing to consider entering the process—on the condition that he pick the team himself, selecting friends of his who were not part of his church and who lived quite a distance away.

Such a Lone Ranger position most likely shows that a person has not truly entered the process of repentance and wants to practice secrecy in order to protect himself. Some of the reasons a person might want to "go it alone" rather than allow his church to become part of the process are these:

☐ Anonymity. If the church doesn't know, I should be able to continue as an elder and Sunday-school teacher.

☐ Less embarrassment. If no one in the church knows, I won't be embarrassed when I see people.

☐ Lack of accountability. If my accountability group is not in the area, and if it's made up of my good friends, I'll more likely be able to "snow them."

☐ Less discipline. If my friends are in charge of disciplining me—and they don't live near me—I'll likely get off more easily.

☐ "Protecting" others. If people in my church knew, it would be awkward for them when they saw me.

As attractive as some of these reasons may appear, they all short-circuit the discipline and restoration process.

What Your Church Can Do Now

From the experience we've gained through working with a number of churches and individuals, we suggest the following steps that could be adopted at the local church level.

1. Policies regarding restoration should be in place ahead of time. Guidelines should be carefully worked out by the church governing body and then presented to the congregation for discussion, modification and approval. This will help the congregation to understand the need and to take responsibility for carrying out the policies.

2. Worship and education time should be given to presentations related to church discipline and restoration issues. We suggest this be done twice a year. It will serve as a reminder to the congregation that each member has a responsibility to lead a holy life and to participate in bringing back to God those who have made sinful choices.

3. Teams should be ready in advance. The local church should actively identify and train members to be able to confront sin while at the same time nurture and care for the sinner. These people should then be incorporated into mature Spiritual Care Teams with experienced members who can continue to mentor them in developing attitudes and skills consistent with the restoration ministry. Appendix A presents specific examples of three local churches that established restoration ministries.

4. Training should be provided for people who wish to be helpful to the victims on a personal level. Victims need our help, just as offenders do. When they are ignored, they withdraw and are lost to the church and sometimes to the kingdom of God. A training session can help team members see things from the family member's point of view so as to better understand what kind of emotional or practical help to offer.

5. Disclosure and confession need to happen as quickly as possible within the church. Pete was senior pastor at a growing church. Before he resigned due to "burnout" (a lie), he had a two-year affair with a parishioner. He confessed the adultery to the church elders when he resigned. Not knowing what to do and not wanting to publicly disgrace the church, the elders decided against a public service for confession.

Pete and his family stayed in town, and he maintained a close relationship with his former congregation. Then his affair became known, so he left the area—but he often returned to visit his family, who stayed there in town. Finally he moved back, in an effort to restore his marriage.

It was now very awkward for Pete and for his family, because no one knew "who knows what, if it's really true, or what the pastor is doing about it if it is." The sooner full disclosure is made, the sooner healing and restoration can begin for all involved.

6. When sin is disclosed, action needs to be taken quickly. We don't wait to take a sick or injured person to a hospital. In the same way, even though an individual's sin may have been going on for months or years, the discovery creates a crisis for the person and the family. However, the crisis can be an opportunity. The disclosure of sin opens up the potential for repentance, forgiveness, healing and restoration. This window of opportunity needs to be carefully guarded, because Satan will try to slam it shut.

The offender may initially experience some relief at disclosure, but these feelings most likely will be accompanied by fear, denial and self-justification. But if a Spiritual Care Team can be formed quickly, this can serve to keep the window of opportunity open so that the fresh air of restoration can freely circulate. Pastors and others whom God may have used to confront the person need to stay in close contact with that individual and the family until a Spiritual Care Team can be put in place.

7. When members leave a church because of sin, every effort should be made to encourage them to face their sin and deal honestly with the people of their new congregation. The purpose is not to ruin someone's reputation but rather to encourage him or her to be honest and return to God. Recently we became painfully aware of a circumstance where a church withheld information from another church's search committee that was evaluating their former pastor. They thought they were doing the new church and the former pastor a favor. They weren't. He returned to his sin, thereby wounding a new congregation. God's kingdom would have been better served if the truth had been told. At that point either the former church or the new church should have offered to provide the pastor with an accountability relationship. If he refused, it would show his unreadiness for the new position.

8. The popular idea of "putting the past behind" must be replaced by the concept of regular spiritual-health checkups. Asking people about their spiritual journey does not show lack of forgiveness—it shows real caring. I've noted that very few people ask me if I am remaining sexually pure and continuing my walk back toward God. Those who do ask are providing a loving ministry to me. They serve as reminders to keep my eyes on the Lord. They are valuable as they show their willingness to be their brother's keeper. Those who don't ask may think they are being kind; instead, they fail to show strong caring. One's past is never over except in God's eyes. Our failures are woven into the fabric of our lives. The sinner can rejoice in God's goodness and forgiveness while at the same time being reminded of his or her own vulnerability and helped to stand against ongoing temptation.

9. The church's ministry of restoration should never be limited to just stopping the sinful behavior. Willful sin takes place in the context of a hardened heart. The local church, through the restoration team, should actively seek to uncover the patterns of thought that have allowed the restoree (consciously or unconsciously) to deny the truth of Scripture regarding holy living. The church must help the restoree identify those beliefs and practices that drew him or her away from God originally. If the cause isn't addressed, the same sin will recur or new sins will surface. We must help the restoree clean the whole house.

Restoration is a family matter for God's family. It will be most effectively guided by the local church. If the church needs help, it can draw on the experience of other congregations or individuals. The important thing is to exercise the faith needed to complete the process.

For many, involvement in restoration may seem frightening or unsafe. Some may worry about being seen as harsh or unforgiving; others may be afraid of judging others lest we also be judged. We don't want to be seen as cruel, as those who "take no prisoners." But the challenge is just the opposite. We must obey God's Word in order to *"leave* no prisoners." Tough yet caring involvement can result in freedom for people who have strayed from God as they receive forgiveness and new purpose as God's beloved children—prisoners no more.

12

Restoration & the Healing Process

*R*estoration and healing are not the same thing. To be restored is to be returned to a place of obedience, blessing and usefulness before God. Healing has to do with recovering from the damage caused by sin. Restoration is related to healing, but it may not occur on the same time schedule, and different concerns may need to be addressed.

Although my personal disaster was the culmination of many sinful choices made over a long period of time, the process of personal healing took longer than any of us ever expected. Months of shame and sorrow were followed by days of depression as I faced the consequences of my sin. These times of depression were followed by fear; my old self-confidence was shattered. Healing in our marriage went through a cycle of progress and decline, progress and decline. At times the commitment was stretched to the limits. Yet the most remarkable thing about the process was God's constant presence.

Five Kinds of Healing

When sinful patterns are uncovered, the consequences of the sin usually come down on the individual with crushing force. A life which may have had the outward appearance of order and togetherness is suddenly shattered, and so are the lives of those close to that person. There is pain—perhaps more pain than the person has ever experienced before. Illusions are destroyed; the person stands uncovered and alone, wondering if he or she will ever experience life in a positive way again.

There are at least five specific areas for healing of which Spiritual Care Team members need to be aware.

1. Loss of support from one's "inner circle." The old certainties are suddenly gone. In my case there were changes in business, professional and ministry relationships as well as in friendship patterns. Some of the people who had "been there" before didn't want to be there any longer. Others who may have wanted to be there and help didn't know how. All of us were immersed in pain and confusion.

My therapist and members of the Spiritual Care Team helped me work through the implication of these losses and evaluate future courses of action. My healing was more complete because those closest to me refused to let me believe that all the pain would blow over and I could go back to business as usual. When we discussed my future it was always with the awareness that it had to be different. My relationships would have to change also. They needed to be based on truth and reality, not deceit and pretense. Sin had to be stopped for complete healing to occur. I discovered that the old certainties needed to go. They were an unstable foundation upon which I had built my life.

2. Depression. A second need for healing relates to the depression which usually accompanies the process of having to face your shameful past. Sometimes I would tell Sandy, "I think I'm depressed today." Usually she would nod in agreement or say, "I think so." Rarely did she try to fix it for me. She understood that depression was an appropriate emotional response to the shambles I had made of our lives.

I had counseled enough people with depression to know that taking steps to face the problems I had created would bring relief. I needed to take steps of obedience to God and to listen to the wise advice being offered by my therapist, the Spiritual Care Team and my wife. Dr. McIvor encouraged me to set goals and work toward them. Spiritual Care Team members acknowledged progress and encouraged me along the path.

3. Fear and shaken identity. When I visited Mark, Betty, Jim and Joan to confess my sins and apologize, I was no longer the proud, self-confident colaborer I had once been. I was confused, afraid, sometimes physically trembling. I knew how to live out the old me but I didn't know what to do with me now. Joan must have sensed my fear. As she and Jim were leaving to go to a church function, she brought me a pile of afghans. "I thought you might like to curl up in these," she said. "It gets a little cold in the house." They tucked me in on the family room couch, said goodby and left. Warmed by their care and the softness of the afghans, I felt safe.

Afghans became the arms of God around me. I still didn't know whom I would become, but I felt the beginning of a new security—in God, not in the person I had been. In the months and years that followed, the Spiritual Care Team nurtured me through further steps of healing in this area. They helped me discover who God wants me to be.

4. Grieving the loss. Another important area of healing is grieving. The more my denial was shattered, the more I grieved over the losses, real and potential, that my sinful choices had caused. Later I grieved because of the losses I had caused my wife and children. I came to realize that their lives would never be the same either. I was sustained in my grief by the prayers of the

Spiritual Care Team. They were grieving too, but they did not draw back from Sandy and me or from our children during this important time of dealing with loss and restarting life. The Spiritual Care Team did more than just attend the "funeral." They helped search for evidence of life amongst the ashes. Some potential losses were avoided, such as loss of our marriage and loss of relationship with the children. But even now there is loss for us all. We all live with pain and are all still grieving.

5. Broken relationships. The fifth area for healing is undoubtedly the biggest and most complex. This is the need for healing in relationships. People were damaged emotionally, socially, financially and in other ways by what I had done. It would have been wrong for me to expect that they just forgive and forget. Believe me, that's what I wanted! However, the important thing for my healing was not to demand or even expect forgiveness but to confess what I had done and acknowledge the need for healing relationships.

Healing within the family was (and is) an ongoing process. Sandy and I tried to talk, but it was difficult. Our foundation had been destroyed. She felt as if she was living with a stranger. She struggled to take care of herself and the children while trying to figure out what to do with me. I struggled with feelings of separation and isolation, and the reality of Sandy's lack of trust hit me hard. When she opened her own bank account I cried out inside. "This just isn't the way things are done! Isn't family income *our* money?" I was insensitive to her need to grasp for some sense of security for herself and the children. I knew I wasn't going to run, but how could she possibly know that? It proved to be important that I not fight the changes Sandy needed to make in order to protect herself. This made it easier for her to relearn trust. The team members helped each of us work through the tests that these changes brought.

Each of the children responded with different needs to the crisis my revelations created. We couldn't pretend that things were all hunky-dory. The myth of the perfect family was exposed. The need for healing within our family was apparent at every turn. Anger and fear needed to be expressed. Instant forgiveness could not be expected. Time, prayer and open communication allow healing to take place. Most of the healing is ongoing. We believe all healing ultimately occurs as God, the Master Physician, touches lives. Spiritual Care Team members have a direct part in the process and play an important role in praying for all involved. They are also useful in helping the restoree to evaluate progress and needs in the ongoing healing process with various family members.

Parental reactions must also be dealt with. They present significant tests of healing. Sandy's mom told me in no uncertain terms how she felt about my adulterous behavior. She expressed her feelings of disgust, betrayal and anger. Sandy wanted to intervene and make it all better for me, but she chose not to. She wisely realized that she could not control what happened between her mom and me. She chose to let us work it out. This is usually the best course of healing.

Parental responses are varied. Parents may accept blame that isn't theirs; they may choose to side with their children; sometimes they side against them. No matter what the reaction, the matter should remain open for discussion so that healing can occur. Sandy's mom and I were on good terms when she died several years later.

The healing of relationships outside the family is often overlooked. Dr. McIvor provided very wise counsel for me in this area. He said, "If you want relationships with people to be restored, you are going to have to take the initiative. You can't expect people who have been hurt by you to come to you." I didn't want to hear this, but I needed to hear it. I was the offender. One by one as people would come to my mind I would make contact. Usually my efforts were rewarded and healing took place between us. Some relationships, though, were lost.

Sandy's input was very important. She regularly got comments from people who had unanswered questions for me. These ranged from expressions of anger to questions such as "How's Earl doing? I care, but I haven't known how to ask."

Sometimes she said to me, "I think you should consider talking to _____. There may be some unfinished business there." More often, however, she said to the person who approached her, "I think it could be helpful to both you and Earl if you'd be willing to discuss your anger and concern with him. I know he'd be open to talking. Why don't you talk to him directly?" Sandy's refusal to be the middle person and her encouragement to people to work through their emotions became a real source of healing. Some losses can be recouped if the restoree and the party who has been hurt are willing to have direct contact. It's always easier to avoid direct contact, but healing rarely results without it.

After five years of no direct contact, I met with a couple, Bill and Susan, with whom I had been friends for years. Our relationship had been strained by my avoidance and by the impact of my sin. It needed healing, and God provided the occasion.

I apologized for the hurt, disillusionment and pain I had caused. My friends shared how they had felt and asked questions to try to clarify their confusion. Clarification led to expressions of forgiveness and encouragement for me. I began to see God healing the relationship and each of us. Susan insightfully said, "It seems that as the result of the ministry you have received from your Spiritual Care Team, you have finally come to a place where you allow people to care for you!" I was amazed as I felt the impact of God's love through this restored relationship.

Undoubtedly there are more areas for healing than we have discussed. Suffice it to say that the needs for healing, both physical and emotional, should be carefully evaluated and addressed.

Healing Functions Performed by the Team

As instruments of healing, the Spiritual Care Team can perform some specific functions which impact healing. We will look at six of the most important ones.

1. Providing direction. The first healing function is providing direction. Restorees know they need healing, but they do not know how to go about getting it. Outside input is invaluable.

Jesus pointed out, "It is not the healthy who need a doctor, but the sick. I have not come to call the righteous, but sinners to repentance" (Lk 5:31-32). The restoree is sick because of sin and needs the attention of a medical team. The restoree cannot heal himself or herself alone; that has been tried time after time without success. In most cases these attempts have resulted in the same confusion expressed by the apostle Paul: "I have the desire to do what is good, but I cannot carry it out. For what I do is not the good I want to do; no, the evil I do not want to do—this I keep on doing" (Rom 7:18-19).

When the prophet Elisha was confronted by the leper Naaman, who cried for healing, he gave him a clear set of directions: "Go, wash yourself seven times in the Jordan, and your flesh will be restored and you will be cleansed" (2 Kings 5:10). The directions didn't make sense to Naaman—they may have even been confusing to Elisha—but they were clearly the directions from the Lord, and after Naaman's servants convinced him to follow these odd instructions, he was healed.

When the Spiritual Care Team directed me not to work for a year, it certainly didn't make sense to me. I thought I was strong again, ready to go back to work. I believed I was well. I reacted to their directive with fear, confusion and anger.

The team had struggled with the decision, but unanimously they had no peace regarding "releasing" me. Paul and Virginia began to wonder, "What have we done?" But time revealed that the "wisdom" of the team was wisdom from God. Going back to work then would have been like having the cast removed from a broken leg and immediately beginning to run two miles a day. I needed more time to heal. Without direction from the team, my healing process might have been short-circuited.

When I told my dad about the sinful life I had been living, he wanted to know what I was doing about it now. He thoughtfully reviewed the process I was going through and the helpers who were alongside. He wanted to know if I was getting proper direction, and if I was following it. Finally he said to me, "Okay, I think you're doing what you need to do."

My dad was aware that we often try to avoid admitting our sickness. Sometimes we don't take our medicine because it reminds us that we are sick. Early in the healing process I had to tell numerous close friends and associates about my sin. It was a necessary part of restoration and healing, but it was bitter medicine. During the early weekly phone conversations with Paul and Virginia, one of them would often ask, "Have you talked to _____ yet?" What they were asking me was, "Are you doing what's necessary for healing?"

They also inquired about rest and exercise. "How are you sleeping?" "Are you getting any exercise?" On the weeks when I traveled to see Dr. McIvor, Virginia and Paul would ask, "How did it go? What help did he offer? What direction did he provide? What concerns did he raise?" In essence they were wanting to know, "What are the doctor's orders? What are the issues for which we need to hold you accountable?"

Following directions is not easy, whether you are a surgical patient, someone who is depressed or a fallen Christian. But it is the only way to healing. Those who provide a ministry of restoration must provide direction.

2. Providing encouragement. A second healing function provided by the team is encouragement. In order to follow directions, restorees need firm but gentle encouragement. Different members of our Spiritual Care Team have different gifts. Nancy observed at one point, "Paul and Virginia shine with an ability to ask the right questions, stand firm in the truth and point toward the future with hope and light. Larry is strong and loyal, always willing to meet with Earl and give support. I'm the friend and prayer warrior. That's the way I encourage."

Even though Sandy was deeply wounded and needing encouragement herself, she did what she could to encourage me. Sometimes it was a gentle squeeze, sometimes a faint smile. Later on she was able to say, "I see you changing and I'm glad."

A vital part of the encouragement process is to point out the visible signs of God's involvement with the restoree on a daily, weekly, monthly, even yearly basis. Healing is a lonely process, and the wounded often lose sight of the Master Healer during times of shame, suffering and readjustment. Early in the process, Virginia said to me on the phone, "I don't think you are suicidal. If you were, you would have ended it already. And I believe you are really trying to do what God wants you to do. You're a real encouragement to me." The message was clear: God is present, we are with you also, and we want you to continue on.

In my mind I keep a list of the various ways God and others have encouraged me over the past few years. It includes:

- ☐ dolphins around the boat to Catalina Island
- ☐ a perfectly timed call from a friend
- ☐ a significant comment from an elder at church
- ☐ specific answers to prayers for encouragement
- ☐ things learned during quiet times with God
- ☐ the confession before the whole church body
- ☐ the marriage recommitment service
- ☐ Sandy falling back in love with me
- ☐ healing conversation with our children
- ☐ ministry from friends in St. Louis
- ☐ the end of the professional probation period

☐ the celebration dinner with the team

☐ new beginnings in my professional practice

☐ new opportunities for service in Romania and at Trinity Western University

3. Dealing with discouragement. Another healing function which is closely related to encouragement is helping the person deal with discouragement. Restorees are rarely lighthearted and cheerful during this painful time. They easily fall prey to discouragement—it is a normal part of the healing process. At first the restoree may be so discouraged or depressed that he or she doesn't want to heal. At other times the person may be discouraged because healing is not taking place fast enough. Discouragement is a phase in adjusting to new realities. The members of the restoration team can aid in the healing process at this point.

A woman named Joan, whose husband had fallen into sin, was being helped by a Spiritual Care Team. She asked her team leader two questions, "Why am I so down? Why is this getting to me so?"

The leaders began by putting things in perspective. "Tell me, Joan, ten years ago could you have ever imagined that you would be sitting here in this little apartment with this group of people trying to help you put your life back together? Did you ever think that you would be working at the near-minimum-wage job that you have? Did you ever think you would be called on to make such far-reaching family decisions—or be so far away from so many people you love so much?" Joan shook her head in silent resignation.

The team members then began to talk with her about the positive side. "God has good things ahead for you, Joan. What do you think God wants you to do now that you have ended up where you are? What are your steps to healing? God is a God of new beginnings; what can you do to cooperate with his work in your life?" Dealing with discouragement is vital to the healing process. Team members can best facilitate the process when they approach it with cautious optimism. People need to be encouraged to believe, but their belief often has to be guided one step at a time. Just saying "It's all going to work out" may feel like hollow encouragement. It may be more useful to point out how God takes people through one step to prepare them for the next.

4. Calling for continued obedience. As I repented, responded to God in obedience and submitted to the directives of the team, a transforming process of healing was begun. There were immediate positive results of obedience, and these encouraged me to continue. Repentance and following my therapist's advice made control of sexual behavior possible. New habits of truth and integrity began to emerge. Self-control and truth-telling were reinforced by Spiritual Care Team members' affirmations, and new positive patterns of life began to emerge.

Obedience was happening—but there were still many things to be learned. When God restores a person, *he restores toward the image of God, not toward the previous best level of the restoree.* This often creates conflict and resistance on the part of the restoree as new areas for obedience surface. For example, it was easier for me to deal with my sexual sin than to address my selfishness and insensitivity. Other restorees have had similar experiences. When Jack was told, "You need to change the way you treat your wife," he stiffened with resistance. It was as though he was thinking, *I already admitted committing adultery; what more do you want from me? I'm not a wife beater—I know I'm not as bad as some other husbands.* Such disclaimers thwart the very purpose of restoration. God doesn't want people to be what they used to be. He doesn't want them just to be better than average. God wants them to be like him. He wants them to be all they can be. Agreeing to this fuller work is a real test of faith. People may feel it is unfair that they have to be "better than" everyone else. *Haven't I gone through enough?* they may ask themselves. God, who heals, has the answer to that question. The answer is, "No. Allow me to complete my work." God can and will complete his work, and the Spiritual Care Team is a resource he will use.

The limitations of healing hinge on the answers to such seemingly innocent questions. The answers that lead to healing are firmly embedded in the book of Romans. "Therefore, I urge you, brothers, in view of God's mercy, to offer your bodies as living sacrifices, holy and pleasing to God—which is your spiritual act of worship. Do not conform any longer to the pattern of this world, but be transformed by the renewing of your mind. Then you will be able to test or approve what God's will is—his good, pleasing and perfect will" (Rom 12:1-2).

Just as an athletic coach promotes continual adherence to proper technique and a music teacher promotes practice as the means to perfect performance, team members need to promote continued obedience. Obedience in the hard places. Obedience in new, previously unexamined areas of life. Obedience that will allow for complete healing.

5. Encouraging openness. Another function of the Spiritual Care Team is to encourage openness on the part of the restoree. Openness leads to healing. We are amazed by the rapid healing that occurs in some athletes following physical injury. What are their secrets? How are they able to return to the playing field so quickly? Do they know some things that we can learn to speed our own healing?

The answers are not so much to be found in specific things they do as in the attitudes they display. There is an openness to input, a teachability that permeates them and propels them to work hard, to follow new suggestions—to do whatever it takes. They are relentless in their pursuit of healing. They are desperate to be pronounced fit to join the game again. So they show little interest in shortcuts. They trust in their physical therapists and follow their orders.

Such openness pays great dividends. In fact, the results are often called miraculous by those who look on. Spiritual Care Team members need to encourage such openness in the restoree. Larry has often challenged me by saying, "Take a look at this," or, "What do you think of that?" He throws in ideas to be considered and tested. It is often the new ideas that serve to further the healing process.

6. Calling the restoree to truth. A final function of the team in promoting healing is continuing to call the restoree to truth. Throughout this book we have taken the stance that without truth-telling there cannot be true healing. But we admit that when the truth is told, the result is often a great trial for the restoree and the family. Our team accepted the role of clarifying and answering questions wherever possible to ensure that public information was correct.

Truth-telling often results in radical changes and lost opportunities. When I went to the dean of the seminary where I was teaching and told him about my sin, I was removed from the classroom, as I should have been. I felt terrible. I didn't want to keep telling the truth.

One pastor confessed his addiction and offered his resignation. The resignation was quickly accepted. Zap—a dozen years' work was over, just like that. No one asked him to stay on or even expressed regret at his leaving. He suffered a great loss; he felt devalued. The shock was great and the change was radical. The internal response to such changes often results in a severe challenge to our faith. At this point the Spiritual Care Team may see withdrawal and resistance on the part of the restoree. They must, however, continue to call for truth if healing is to occur. Anything less will abort the process and leave the individual unrestored and unhealed.

I must confess that when first confronted with my sin, I didn't want to be restored or healed. I wanted things to be the way they had always been, and I didn't want to hurt. Following my desires would not have resulted in either restoration or healing.

I am thankful that God and my Spiritual Care Team required more of me. I followed some simple rules which created a cognitive bridge to my healing.

☐ Follow the doctor's orders.

☐ Take your medicine.

☐ Get plenty of rest.

☐ Be patient—take life one day at a time.

☐ Do the things that God lays out for you to do.

☐ Allow God's people, your friends, to minister to you.

☐ Learn to live with setbacks.

☐ Broaden your boundaries of obedience.

☐ Remain open to new input.

At first I didn't want to be healed. I just wanted to be pain-free. I would have settled for pain control when effective treatment was available. At times I needed surgery as sinful conditions needed to be removed.

Yes, it was difficult, but it is wonderful to see how different my life is now. Recently I told Sandy and the Spiritual Care Team I am so thankful that I'm where I am instead of where I was heading. I'm alive!

13

Aftercare

In December 1992, after Earl had spent a year unemployed at the direction of the Spiritual Care Team, the team met to evaluate his progress. We unanimously concluded that the goals of the restoration process had been met over this three-year period.

I vividly remember meeting with the team in December 1992. It was the culmination of the third year of my restoration process —the year in which I had not worked, in compliance with the team's direction. I had concentrated on learning to be alone with God and learning to serve Sandy, the children and others. It had been a great year—one I will never forget. Spiritually, I had begun to learn to be comfortable in God's presence: praying, reflecting, sitting still. Practically, I had learned to help around the house. I had even learned to cook! This was a way I could serve the family, since Sandy was working full-time.

To mark the conclusion of the formal restoration process,

Larry took the six of us out for a celebration dinner, and we reviewed the wonderful things God had done. It was a time of thanking God and for Sandy and me to express thanks to the team. We talked about how our relationships might change after this evening. I knew that Paul and Virginia wouldn't stop calling and writing, but those calls wouldn't be as often as before. I also knew that Sandy and I were free to call for fellowship, advice or prayer as we felt the need. We would miss our quarterly face-to-face meetings, but even that evening we were trying to plan a time to get together again.

Tears filled my eyes as Paul spoke of the role of the team in my life-changing process. I realized with joy how important this process had been. But now a new step was about to be taken. The team was placing the control panel of my life back in my hand. I was excited, but the excitement was mixed with fear. Was I stable enough to make only those choices that would honor Christ? I had practiced spiritual disciplines; would I maintain them if no one was holding my feet to the fire? Would I get so involved in rebuilding my professional practice and career that I would neglect serving others? The team thought I was ready. I asked myself, *Am I really ready?*

Aftercare is the ongoing process of caring for the restoree after the period of formal restoration has been completed. Special medical care for surgery patients does not end when they are released from the hospital after the operation. Similarly, the need for care for the restoree does not end with a declaration of restoration. In both instances care is still needed, but the intensity and methods of care change.

As we have seen personally how crucial good aftercare is, we have isolated a number of key issues upon which aftercare should focus.

Provide Ongoing Accountability

The need for accountability after the formal restoration process is finished should not be overlooked—it is critical. Restoration does not mean that temptations are gone, that weakness had been eliminated or that the newly acquired positive patterns won't wane. All of these areas need to be closely monitored. Often the restoration process reveals the need for an even broader base of accountability. Dr. McIvor had told me that my period of greatest sexual vulnerability would probably occur after much of the initial pain had subsided, when I was released from the intense scrutiny of therapy and of the Spiritual Care Team, and when my life began to return to normalcy. In my case it was important to focus on issues such as pace of life and spiritual disciplines as well as issues related to sexual purity and my relationship with Sandy and our children.

Larry was asked to monitor my schedule and be at the front when decisions regarding opportunities for ministry might arise. Larry and I decided to meet regularly, as schedules allowed, to share prayer requests and fellowship together. Larry also volunteered to be available to accompany me to any speaking engagements so that he could encourage and support me as well as evaluate what I said. Because deception and lying by omission were significant areas of sin for me, it was important that I not return to those patterns. Larry would keep an ear out for them.

Monitor Attitudes and Behavior
New attitudes and behaviors are usually tentative and vulnerable to erosion. They must be practiced on a regular basis or the old, more familiar (although inappropriate) patterns will reemerge. The informal contacts that occur between the restoree and the team members provide opportunities for monitoring: encouraging the new, appropriate behavior and asking questions when evidence of old patterns emerges. "Earl, that sounds to me like glossing over again," Virginia stated one day. "Are you aware that you are doing that?" An important follow-up discussion took place.

Sandy also participates in monitoring, providing both encouragement and challenges. "I see you being really open with the kids," she observed once. "I think you're making headway." On another occasion she remarked, "I feel like you're shaving the truth again. It makes me feel uncomfortable."

Monitoring is like taking vital signs in the hospital. It helps the doctor know what preventive or corrective steps to take. Monitoring can also provide the restoree with information needed to stay on track with the new behavior and to avoid relapses.

A telephone call from one of our friends illustrates how helpful monitoring can be. Betty said, "I need to talk to you about some concerns I have. Do you have some time?" A meeting was arranged for later that week.

Betty told me, "I have taken seriously your challenge to be our brother's keeper, so I need to share something I have observed you doing lately that has concerned me. You have been real lax in returning phone calls, and I'm worried that you could slip into some old patterns." Not returning telephone calls could be related to being too stressed, to general disregard for others—or even to old patterns of deceit.

After hearing Betty's concern, I agreed that it was correct and that continuing to act in that manner could be hurtful. I promised to work on my laxity right away. Betty's monitoring provided information and resulted in motivation for establishing new habits. Betty had indeed been her brother's keeper, and this became an important part of the aftercare process.

Keep On Providing Support

The patterns of behavior associated with the sinful state have to be dismantled during the restoration process. This dismantling is painful and usually leaves the restoree feeling uncertain and insecure. The insecurities do not go away easily or quickly, and the process of finding new assurances and security in God takes time. One of the purposes of the aftercare process is to see that the restoree does not grow weary in well-doing. During our weekly meetings Larry would often say things like "I'm liking what I'm seeing," "That's progress!" or "You need to take care of this." His presence became a constant reminder to me to stay on target and not lose hope. When I would express fears, Larry was there to provide prayer and other support or sometimes a push in the right direction.

The physical presence of a caring person is in itself a great source of support. Restorees are often isolated or isolate themselves at a time when they need people the most. Meeting regularly to offer support can provide the restoree with a visual reminder of God's presence.

At one time or another all the members of the restoration team had occasion to encourage both Sandy and me in our rebuilding process. Telephone calls, cards, reminders of prayer and expression of love and affection arrived in a timely manner and were always welcome. Continued involvement by the team members after the formal process was a reminder that the restoration process was more than just a project. After contact with one of the team members, I would often find myself thinking, *God sure is taking good care of me! I don't deserve it, but I'm sure thankful.*

Bridges Back to the Community
Wherever sin occurs there are breakdowns in relationships. Whenever restoration occurs there is a need to be building bridges and restoring relationships. The primary responsibility for rebuilding relationships remains with the restoree. During the course of therapy, Dr. McIvor reminded me of this important truth. "Many people have been hurt and disillusioned by what you have done. You cannot expect these people to come to you. If you value the relationships, you need to go to them. It's your choice. It's your responsibility."

Systematically I tried to follow this advice by being open about what I had done and by apologizing to individuals who came to mind or crossed my path. Because I have a wide sphere of contact, I need to continue even now, when I meet someone I haven't talked with about my sin, to be open and to accept responsibility for hurts I may have caused that person.

Paul reflects, "Time after time people would come up to me and ask how Earl was doing. Just as it was important to be honest about Earl's sin to those who asked, it was equally important to speak honestly about the discipline and restoration going on in Earl's life. With great joy I have had the privilege of sharing the story of repentance, discipline and restoration with many who had assumed that Earl and Sandy were divorced, were not doing well or might have turned away from their faith. It was wonderful to be able to be the bearer of good news that became a source of encouragement to a number of people."

One unexpected aspect of building bridges back to the community had to do with a rumor that started four years after the disclosure.

When I returned to my office one afternoon there was a message to call Paul. A daytime call was unusual. I wondered what was so important that Paul would call when higher rates were in effect. I returned the call, and soon Paul was asking a hard question, but one that had been asked before. "Have you had sex with any clients other than the one who brought the complaint?"

I said, "No. You know about *all* of my sexual involvement."

Paul then told me about a rumor that I had been sexually inappropriate with other clients. He asked for permission to follow up on it. I said yes without hesitation and expressed gratitude that he would spend even more of his valuable time on my behalf. He said he would call me when he had more information and he would also call Sandy.

I remember trembling as I hung up the telephone. *Is there ever going to be an end to this?* My next thought was to call Sandy. I realized what a blow this could be to the trust which had been developing. What if the rumor could not be disproved? I knew this would open up old wounds. I had lied too many times in the past.

I called her. I felt her withdraw as the words fell off my lips. She was shaken. I told her that Paul would call her later. Neither of us knew what to say. "I'll talk to you tonight," I said. "Goodby." A fog of silence and fear filled the office.

During the next couple of weeks Paul talked to Sandy, Larry and Nancy; all of us prayed as Paul worked to trace the rumor. *Please, God,* I pleaded, *extend your mercy so that the truth will be substantiated.*

During that month the team had its scheduled meeting at Paul and Virginia's. It was apparent to all that Sandy was still in pain. I sat crying as the team ministered to her and prayed for her resilience. I was so grateful that we had access to this loving aftercare as we worked toward complete healing.

God was faithful, and the source of the rumor was found. There had been an incorrect communication. When the person who had misunderstood what he heard was confronted, he took responsibility for the mistake and agreed to correct the error with those he had told. A sense of relief and rejoicing prevailed.

Monitor Rebuilding Within the Family

Each time Larry and I get together, Larry asks about Sandy and the children (they are adults now, but they are still our kids). He wants to know what's happening in various relationships. He wants to know how he can support our family members in prayer. He, Nancy, Paul and Virginia also call Sandy to get information and provide encouragement firsthand. Their calls are always appreciated, as are their prayers. On several occasions there has been opportunity to see the children and encourage them. It is all part of aftercare.

When the formal responsibility of the team is completed, it is as though a safety net has been removed for the family members. Old fears can be rekindled. The spouse and children wonder if progress will continue once the support of the team has been lessened or removed. As the restoree begins to step out independently again, family members may wonder, *Has he really changed? Will the new commitments remain firm? Will the deceit and lying start all over again?*

Sandy wondered if she would be able to stand up to me during those times when I would refuse to hear her. Whom could she go to for support? The grown children watched to see what was happening with our marriage. They had difficulty trying to interpret the meaning of disagreements. On one occasion one of them said, "You'd better talk to Paul and Virginia about this." An important part of aftercare is keeping open lines of communication and remaining available. The Spiritual Care Team needs to continue to monitor the progress of the restoree through the eyes of the family. This can be accomplished as natural contacts are made with family members.

Provide Ongoing Prayer Support

All of the members of the team are conscious of the desire of the enemy to gain a foothold that would allow him to destroy the restoration which has occurred. Prayer continues to be a powerful defense against such a failure. Nancy reflects upon this important area:

> As much as we wanted to say, "He's well! We're finished! It's over!" we knew that wasn't realistic. When a person's restoration process is completed, our tendency is to assume the work is done. However, throughout Scripture there are warnings to protect us from falling into these kinds of lax attitudes. In 1 Peter 5:8 [NASB] we read, "Be of sober spirit, be on the alert. Your adversary, the devil, prowls about like a roaring lion, seeking someone to devour."

Further warning and instruction can be found in Ephesians 6:18 [NASB]: "With all prayer and petition pray at all times in the Spirit, and with this in view, be on the alert with all perseverance and petition for all the saints."

Because we are and always will be vulnerable to temptation, we need the power of prayer. The Spiritual Care Team realizes this, and our prayers continue to cover the needs of Earl, Sandy and the other team members. A straightforward formula for a successful continual care program is found in 1 Thessalonians 5:16-18 [NASB]: "Rejoice always; pray without ceasing; in everything give thanks." Praise to God serves as the foundation for all prayers and gives us strength and encouragement for future victory.

Aftercare is a vital part of the restoration process and needs to be built into the plan. Ongoing communication and prayer after restoration is completed are vital parts of the process. These proactive steps must be addressed before the team adjourns.

The restoree is not only one who is vulnerable to failure. We are all vulnerable—particularly after a long, hard-fought battle. The effort put forth by the Spiritual Care Team and their families engages them in ongoing spiritual warfare. Prayer is definitely an essential part of aftercare.

14

Restored to Full Ministry?

This chapter was written by Paul Friesen, leader of the Spiritual Care Team. It summarizes the convictions of the team members.

From the very beginning of the discipline and restoration process, we wrestled with the questions "What does 'full' restoration look like? Is there a place for restoration to 'full' ministry after adultery and deceit? What will the end product be?"

We felt the restoration of Earl's relationship with God was foundational. Earl's pattern of dishonesty and sexual sin had taken him to a place quite distant from the relationship God desires.

We were hopeful that someday Sandy and Earl would be restored and again enjoy the intimacy in their marriage that God designed. There was no question that restoring trust between Earl and Sandy and between Earl and his children were legitimate aims. There was also no question that restoration to the local church was within God's purpose. When it came to the question of full restoration to the work of ministry, however, the answer was less obvious.

We did a lot of reading. Most authors seemed to agree that the goal of restoration to fellowship in the local church was within God's plan. But was there the possibility of full restoration to active ministry in the church in a formal sense, or was Earl to be permanently disqualified from any leadership role?

Looking to the opinions of Bible scholars failed to answer the question, since well-respected authorities stood firmly on each side of the subject. Thus we dug into the Scriptures ourselves to see what God was saying to us through his Word regarding the full restoration of Christian leaders to positions of responsibility and authority in the body.

The anchor text for the restoration process seemed like a good place to start. The apostle Paul exhorts "those who are spiritual" to restore the fallen brother (Gal 6:1). The Greek word for *restore* means "to mend." It is interesting to note that there are no disclaimers here and that the types of sins are not specified. It doesn't say "restore unless the person has sinned sexually" or "restore to fellowship but not leadership." It simply tells us to restore.

Inherent in the word *restore* is the idea of bringing back to the original state. One would not be very pleased to take an antique caned-seat chair in for restoration and have the finished product be a chair with a Naugahyde cushion! There is nothing wrong with Naugahyde cushions, but that is not considered restoration if your original chair had a caned seat. The goal is to restore at least to the original condition—as it was before deterioration began.

Apart from our theological conclusions about full restoration, we must examine what is prudent in the life of the congregation and in the life of the fallen individual. If a fallen brother or sister has a long history of child abuse, for instance, it most likely will not be in anyone's best interest—even after repentance and healing occur—to restore him or her to full service in the area of ministry to children.

In *Betrayal of Trust* the authors state, "For some offenders, including predators, restoration to leadership and public ministry will likely never be possible" (Roy D. Bell and Stanley J. Grenz [Downers Grove, Ill.: InterVarsity Press, 1995], p. 172). This does not mean that the fallen person will never be restored to ministry of any kind, but it does say that "full" restoration does not necessarily mean restoration to *all* forms of ministry.

Hebrews 12:12-13 states, "Therefore, strengthen your feeble arms and weak knees. 'Make level paths for your feet,' so that the lame may not be disabled, but rather healed." Healing comes by "making level paths for your feet" and avoiding those things that might trip you up because of your own weakness or the terrain's ruggedness. In 2 Timothy 2:22 we are told to flee the evil desires of youth and pursue righteousness. It is a wise individual who acknowledges an area of weakness and stays clear of it.

When I was in college, we had two students living with our family. Both had significant struggles with sexual lust. One of them, admitting his struggle, refused to go to beach parties with our college group because he didn't feel it would be wise to expose himself to such temptation. Some of the others made fun of him, including his roommate, who stated confidently that he could handle it. The student who had stayed home from the beach parties eventually married and is presently enjoying a healthy family life. The roommate, who did go to the parties, has spent time in prison for committing sexual offenses.

James 1 tells us to *endure trials,* while the apostle Paul tells us in 1 Timothy to *flee from temptation.* Too often we get it backwards: we flee from the trials and endure the temptation—to our own hurt. The church does no one a favor by restoring a leader to a position in which he or she will constantly face the same temptations that led to his or her fall.

Those who object to full restoration to leadership in all cases often refer to 1 Timothy 3:2, which states that a deacon must be "above reproach." What does this mean? If "above reproach" means that a deacon has not sinned in the past in any of the ways listed in 1 Timothy 3:2, we would have very brief deacons' meetings, because no one would be in attendance! If the list were taken too literally, we would not allow anyone to serve on a deacons' board who had ever been quarrelsome, quick-tempered, greedy, inhospitable, drunk or lacking in self-control.

What, then, is this 1 Timothy passage saying about qualifications for those in leadership in the church? Certainly it means that such actions or attitudes must not currently be part of the deacon's life nor have been patterns in the recent past.

We are in no way advocating lowering the high call and qualifications of those in leadership in the church. We too are appalled by the "quick and simple" restoration to leadership we often see today. Restoration is a process, not an instantaneous event. Before an old chair can be restored, it is stripped down to bare wood. Before a Christian leader is able to be restored, he or she must in repentance be "stripped" down to the bare person—and then, in humility, be restored by the Spirit of God working through others. One indication of whether a person is ready for restoration is his or her humility and lack of self-promotion. A truly repentant person knows that restoration must always be declared complete by the brethren, never by the fallen sinner. Those who have walked closely beside the restoree for an extended period of time are in the best position to determine if or when a return to ministry is appropriate.

Situations where notable public Christian figures have pronounced themselves healed seem to be a demonstration more of independence, arrogance and pride than of genuine healing. The

Spiritual Care Team was actively involved with Earl for three years before he was restored to limited ministry. At the end of two years, he thought he had done all that was expected of him, and he felt ready to resume public speaking and writing. But the whole Spiritual Care Team felt that he was not yet ready.

Earl reflects, "I was terribly disappointed—and initially very angry. But after about three days I acquiesced, because by now I trusted the team more than I trusted my own judgment. And I believed that God was working through them to provide direction for my life."

One of the team members noted, "Our consensus was very difficult for Earl to accept at first, but, as had been his pattern, he submitted to our directions even though he did not like them. The third year proved to be the most significant year of the whole process as Earl really devoted himself to his personal spiritual renewal. At the end of the third year we told Earl we felt he was ready to slowly begin formal involvement in ministry. His weeping upon hearing the decision was a spontaneous response to the grace of God expressed through the Spiritual Care Team that day."

Take Enough Time

The length of time for the restoration process will vary with each individual. The longer and more deeply ingrained the pattern of sin, the longer the restoration process will take. The goal of restoration is not to have a clean slate for ninety days but to have a heart that has genuinely been changed. Just as a new believer should not be put in leadership, so a newly restored person should not be released for leadership without establishing a track record of a changed heart and actions. This often takes years, not weeks or months, and it is better to err by requiring extra time rather than by seeking a hasty resolution.

Our daughter recently had foot surgery. The doctor estimated that surgery would last about an hour, but due to some complications it lasted over two hours. We were very thankful that the doctor didn't look at his watch and say, "Time's up. According to the medical journal, this surgery should take only one hour. Go ahead and sew her up." The doctor stayed and worked until the surgery was complete. So it is with restoration. The timing of a return to ministry (if that is the clear direction in which God is leading) is determined by the extent of surgery and the time needed to heal. As each surgery is unique, so each case of restoration is unique. Not all restoration efforts lead back to full-time ministry. If returning to full-time ministry is the driving force behind a person's desire for restoration, it is likely that true restoration is not happening. The driving force must be complete restoration to a right relationship with the Lord. It is indeed a time of starting over, a time of following God to a renewed relationship.

Another passage often used by those opposed to full restoration, specifically for those involved in sexual sin, is 1 Corinthians 6:18: "Flee from sexual immorality. All other sins a man commits are outside his body, but he who sins sexually sins against his own body." This passage singles out sexual immorality and describes the damage this sin does to the body. But it is interesting to note that while the passage talks about the seriousness of the sin, it does not even imply that the sin cannot be forgiven. And there is no footnote indicating a different treatment toward leaders who are involved in this sin. Some will argue that forgiveness is different from restoration and that they are not advocating withholding forgiveness, only restoration. We fail to see a scriptural basis for separating the two.

Welcomed Back

Luke 15:11-32 records a beautiful story of full restoration. The prodigal son left his father, taking his half of the inheritance, and entered fully into a life of sin. He seemed to enjoy this life until the money ran out and he finally "came to his senses."

Destitute, he realized that his father's hired men had it better than he did. So he decided to head back to his father's home to become a hired hand, since he certainly had forfeited the position of sonship.

One day the father was out looking down the road, as he had done on many occasions in hopes that his son would return. From a distance he recognized the step and shape of the figure on the horizon. He ran out and embraced the boy. Before his son had time to finish his rehearsed confession, the father ordered a banquet to be thrown in honor of his son, who "was dead and is alive again, he was lost and is found."

Much to the displeasure of the older son, the younger brother was restored to full sonship, with all the privileges of a son. It is critical to see the difference between the son's being restored to full sonship and the son's having to deal with the consequences of his sin. It is true that his *condition* was far from ideal: he no longer had his inheritance, and perhaps he suffered from worms or other diseases from his time spent with the swine and in other activities. But his *position* was restored: he was still the father's dear son.

Our heavenly Father is always looking down the road for wayward children, because the heart of the Father longs to see his children come home and be restored as full sons and daughters.

Let's look further at the actual restoration of two men in Scripture to positions of leadership after they had committed serious moral sins which became publicly known.

Peter: Coward and Liar

I smile when I read of Peter, because, like so many of us, he was often putting his foot in his mouth. His remarks could often be labeled impulsive and harmless. On one occasion, however, Peter's remarks were quite public and very harmful—when Peter publicly denied the Lord.

This is one of those stories that God seems to want to make sure we hear—it occurs in all four Gospels (Mt 26:69-75; Mk 14:66-72; Lk 22:56-62; Jn 18:16-18, 25-27). Peter publicly denied, three times, that he knew Jesus. Then he went out and "wept bitterly." He was repentant, but the damage had been done. The word was out—Peter had denied that he ever knew Jesus. It would seem that Peter's career with Jesus was over. This significant moral failure—lying, deceiving, denying—would surely signal the end of his leadership position.

Shortly after his resurrection, Jesus commissioned leaders to direct the church after he ascended to heaven. Jesus could have chosen a philosopher who could relate primarily to the world's elite. He could have chosen a "politically correct" person who carefully selected his words so no one would be offended. He could have chosen one who was raised in a good home, who had always been obedient as a child and as an adult had never participated in any wrongdoing of any magnitude. Instead he chose Peter, a fisherman, one who could identify with the common person, one who often spoke his mind before thinking how he might sound, one who had denied the Lord publicly, one like us, who knew right from wrong but didn't always do the right thing.

Perhaps the Lord's decision to choose Peter was based on the fact that he saw beyond Peter's actions into his heart. Jesus knew how important it would be to have one leading the church who had experienced grace at such a deep level that he could lead the early church to be "grace givers."

David: Adulterer and Murderer

There is no more powerful example of full restoration of a leader in the Scriptures than King David. David—harp-playing shepherd boy, chosen by God to be king, destined to be part of the lineage of Jesus, prolific writer of worship songs (and Scripture), mouthpiece of God, man after God's own heart. David—adulterer, deceiver, murderer (1 Sam 16—31; 2 Sam 1—24).

Some people discount David as a valid example of full restoration. They cite the death of his first son, conceived in adultery with Bathsheba, the ongoing family turmoil, the great national trials as indications that God did not bless David's leadership after he sinned (2 Sam 12). These events demonstrate the results of sin in David's life, but they do not in any way indicate his elimination from leadership.

A restored minister told me that hardly a day goes by when he doesn't in some way bear the consequences of his past sinful choices. That does not mean in any way that God's hand of blessing in ministry has been removed from this leader. God has restored and blessed him. Yet he still must deal with the consequences of his sin.

Here are five ways in which David's story shows us that God is a God of full restoration to those who repent:

1. David was not removed from the position of king after his affair, deception and murder. Yes, there were significant difficulties in his kingdom, but God did not rip the throne away from him.

2. Those portions of Scripture written by David prior to his sin were retained as part of the inspired Word of God. God did not "pull the book from the shelves" after David's sin.

3. God allowed David to write other Scriptures after his adultery, deception and murder. David's psalms describing the process of repentance and restoration are some of the most gripping portions of Scripture.

4. David's armies were victorious in battle when David was leading them—after his sin (2 Sam 12:29-31).

5. When David's life was over, his epitaph from God was "David, a man after God's own heart" (1 Sam 13:14; Acts 13:22).

Since there do not appear to be any Scripture passages that specifically prohibit fallen leaders from being fully restored to ministry, and since some examples of fallen leaders in Scripture are examples of restoration, we must be very hesitant to forbid full restoration of leaders to appropriate ministry after discipline and after restoration to God and others.

Further, if a church takes the position that a leader can never be fully restored due to significant sin, it tends to foster hiding rather than honesty. This is especially damaging in the early stages of sin. When a leader is tempted, his or her response could be changed if he or she could confess the temptation (or the first occurrence of sin) to the board of elders or an accountability group. But when the church's position is that anyone in leadership should never struggle with such things, the leader may choose to go into hiding and deal with it alone. That often leads to deeper involvement in the sin and its destructive patterns.

There is no question that early detection of diseases saves lives. So it is with sin. Early detection and treatment can keep sin from developing fully and causing death to the sinner. We are able to come to God for help because we have a High Priest who understands our temptations and urges us to come to the throne of grace boldly to receive mercy (Heb 4:15-16). We come to a God who wants to extend mercy and grace, not condemnation and judgment. How wonderful it would be if a fellow believer, when tempted or fallen, would voluntarily come boldly (not arrogantly, but confident of God's and the church's help) to the church to receive mercy and grace.

In James 5:16 we are told, "Confess your sins to each other and pray for each other so that you may be healed." We are urged to confess not that we may be destroyed or sidelined forever, but that we may be healed. The church must become a safe place for believers to be real and not play the "appearance-management" game for fear someone might discover their faults. *If we are to be a healing body, we must be a confessing body.*

When Jesus was awaiting his execution, all the disciples denied him—either by their spoken words, as Peter did, or by their silence. How wonderful that Jesus did not eliminate those men from leadership because they buckled under the pressure at a critical time! Jesus saw fit to restore the disciples and empower them to full leadership. How can we do any less for the repentant sinner in our midst? Those of us in leadership today are there not because we are without sin but because we are recipients of the Father's great mercy and grace.

Two Kings and Their Orchestras

There once was a king who loved music. He had the musicians of his kingdom perform for him nightly, and music filled the castle. But any musician who made a mistake was kicked out of the castle and never allowed to return. The remaining players were terrified that they too might make a mistake, and their preoccupation with this fear seemed to incline them to do the very thing they feared most. More and more were expelled. As the years went by fewer and fewer people learned to play instruments, so terrified were they of failing before the king. Finally, after a number of years, the king spent every night in a silent castle. There were no musical errors, no off-key notes played—because there were no musicians left to play. The castle was void of music.

In a neighboring kingdom there lived a king who also loved music. He too had his subjects perform for him. When they made a mistake, he also asked them to leave. The difference was that he asked them to go and see his chief musician so they could learn from their mistakes, improve in their abilities and return to the orchestra. To this day, in his castle, there is beautiful music heard nightly as the "restored" musicians together make music that flows out of love, not fear.

May God help us to be those who instruct, encourage, discipline and restore those "playing in the King's orchestra" so that the melodies may become more and more beautiful and majestic each day. And may we each, by God's grace and the extended grace of the body, be found in that great collection of forgiven and restored musicians who play and sing to the glory of God out of the riches of his grace.

Epilogue

Looking Back (A Message from the Team)

As we reflect on the last seven years, we are filled with thanksgiving for all God has done in Earl's life. Earl is closer to the Lord today than he was seven years ago; he is closer to his wife; he is closer to his family. Earl is living life in freedom and light after years of living in bondage and darkness. We can truly say that what Satan meant for evil, God has used for good.

But does it have to be that way? Does the prescription for vital spiritual life necessitate a major fall—a Humpty Dumpty experience? a dance with evil? Is Earl better off because he partnered with Satan by engaging in an ungodly lifestyle? "Shall we go on sinning so grace may increase?" (Rom 6:1). No. God's way is the best way: avoidance of sin, pursuit of truth, and the pleasure of fellowship with the Lord.

God in his mercy provided a way of escape for Earl from his lifestyle of sin (1 Cor 10:13). The letter sent by the Oregon Board of Psychologist Examiners which led to a period of probation was a "severe mercy." It contained an accurate, detailed pinpointing of Earl's sin and unethical behavior. It exposed his double life so that he could no longer avoid dealing with it. From a human standpoint the letter promised to destroy Earl's life and livelihood; from a spiritual standpoint it was the merciful intervention of truth that began the process of liberating Earl from a bondage that would destroy him if left unchecked.

Earl's life has been rebuilt, refocused and renewed. He has chosen to be sexually clean for over seven years. Someone might be tempted to think, *If things work out so well after an escapade with sin, why not engage in it myself?* Such thinking clearly ignores the mandate of Scripture for us to live holy lives. It makes a mockery of the life of daily fellowship with the heavenly Father. It does not consider the tremendous pain that sin causes to God, to the sinner, to those whose lives have been shattered by the actions, and to those who watch in agony and confusion.

King David learned anew of the grace of God after his repentance from adultery, deception and murder. But David was not "better off" after his forays into sin. He was forgiven; he was used by God; he wrote many psalms after his fall; he continued to lead his people. But some effects of his sinful choices stayed with him for life. That will be true for Earl as well. Consequences are not obliterated by forgiveness. Some of the effects of his sin will be with Earl all the days of his life.

We have been involved with a number of couples who are rebuilding their marriages after major involvement in sin has become evident. Pain describes everyone's lot—pain, suffering, confusion, betrayal, hurt, rejection. The days of recovery are long and hard; often they feel as though they will never get through the pain. Knowing of all the destruction that sin such as adultery brings and all the grace that God affords, would we choose a life that leads to destruction and then is redeemed by grace, or a life that avoids the pain of sin's entanglement in the first place?

A student who was raised in a Christian home told Paul how he got caught in the trap of "glorified sin." Jim toed the line as he grew up, doing what his parents expected and being a "good Christian boy." He listened to testimonies of the drug addicts, the sex addicts, the "bad boys" whose lives had been transformed by the gospel. The testimonies all recounted the sinfulness of their lives before Christ and the transformation they experienced in coming to faith. They all claimed to have wonderful lives "ever since." Jim decided, *If things are wonderful afterward, why shouldn't I experience the thrill of sin and then repent?*

He looked Paul straight in the eye and said, "I was deceived. They lied. It isn't all 'wonderful ever since.' I have memories. I have hurt many people. I have lost respect for myself. I have shame to deal with. It's *not* all 'wonderful ever since.' "

The thrust of this book is how to care for those who have fallen into sin. Our prayer is that as more churches understand and use the principles of honesty and accountability, fewer and fewer will need this book—because they will have participated more fully in preventive medicine, thereby lessening the need for crisis care and intervention. For if God in his grace and mercy is powerful enough to restore fallen brothers and sisters, he surely is powerful enough to prevent them from falling in the first place.

Let us never cease giving God praise for his wonderful expression of mercy and grace in our lives as fallen people. May we day by day make the personal choice to live, and encourage others to live, a life marked by obedience and intimacy with God.

Appendix A

Spiritual Care Teams in Other Churches

*A*s *the work of our* Spiritual Care Team became known, many people began to observe the process and ask questions. It became apparent that we were engaged in a process about which very little is known. When our team members sought counsel from others whom they thought to be experienced, they found themselves in the role of consultant rather than consultee. Pastors and other Christian leaders often made comments such as "Our church had a similar situation, and we didn't know how to handle it."

When Sandy and I were asked to describe the help we were receiving, we often heard comments like "Wow! The people I know who have fallen haven't received any help like *that!*"

During the past seven years, all six of our team members have been asked to be involved in the establishment of other teams. Some of these efforts have been successful; some are still in process; some have been unsuccessful.

Each of the three case studies we present here is unique. Each shows at least some degree of success. We share the experiences of those involved in some detail in order to provide a first-hand glimpse of the strengths and difficulties of the model. In all three cases we include direct quotes from team leaders as examples of how to get started, how to proceed and how to finish. Although we have stressed the importance of honesty and avoidance of cover-up throughout this book, we have changed the names of the individuals and churches discussed in this section.

The Neighboring-State Church
In early 1992 John Smith, the senior pastor of a church in a neighboring state, resigned, confessing that he had been involved in the heavy use of alcohol and the misuse of prescription medications. He also confessed that he was addicted to gambling. At the time of his resignation, John asked the church to guide him in a restoration process and demonstrated a willingness to submit himself to the authority of the church. The chairman of the church board recalls,

> We as a leadership group made a commitment to be extremely open with and vulnerable to our people—something that is really the norm for us. We also, in those first months, were extremely concerned with the strong possibility of a church split. John was loved by many (some of whom said, "What's the big deal about a little problem with drinking and gambling?" and "He couldn't help it. It's not a sin problem; it's an addiction"), but there was also a group that was pushing for an immediate and complete separation of the church from the pastor. We saw these differing views even within our leadership.

The church did not have a clear-cut model of restoration to follow, so they sought help from a well-known and trusted Christian leader. That person eventually contacted Sandy and me to see if we would help. I contacted the local church board to discuss their situation and to offer our assistance. John and his family were moving close to Portland, so it was agreed that I should call him, present the idea of a Spiritual Care Team and assist in establishing a team, which Sandy and I would lead. The local church agreed to support the team in every way possible and to continue to provide for the family in practical ways such as maintaining their health insurance, assisting with their move and monitoring the sale of their house.

I met with one of the elders from the church within the first two weeks, and we made plans to formulate a local team. We agreed to get suggestions from John and his wife, Joan, regarding prospective team members. Then we began to make contacts. As the process was prayerfully nurtured, God led two other couples to join us, and we began to meet.

The first meeting was held in May 1992. An elder from the out-of-state church traveled to the meeting to show support for the team and to assist in establishing a working relationship between the team and the church. We were all concerned about assisting in the pastor's restoration process and also about facilitating the healing that needed to take place in the now pastorless church. Close communication between the restoration team and the hurting local church was a priority.

For the first year and a half the Spiritual Care Team focused on the physical and emotional health problems that John was experiencing and on addressing the practical problems that had resulted from his sinful choices. John was so severely depressed that he was minimally responsive to the team's guidance. He was deeply immersed in shame and feelings of uselessness. His wife was overwhelmed with the load of responsibilities that she was now forced to carry. An adult son, who had been quite dependent on his parents, was suddenly placed in a position of having to be strong and having his parents dependent on him for emotional support.

Another son and his wife were isolated from the parents and the restoration process both geographically and emotionally. Some unresolved issues arose for them as the result of their father's moral failure. The local church attempted to keep in contact with them, and I established contact via telephone. Unfortunately, the Spiritual Care Team was not able to provide any type of direct ministry to them.

The following summary, provided for the local church body by the elders, describes the restoration process:

In the early months of 1992, the leadership of our church determined the need and publicly committed to come alongside John and Joan Smith in order to be a partner with them in their process of restoration. We declared our desire and commitment to be a part of (1) their restoration to fellowship with God, (2) their restoration to fellowship with our local body of believers and (3) their restoration to Christian service. We concluded, though, that John's restoration to Christian leadership would have to be clearly directed by God and would require John's submission to an extended time for testing and proving his character.

An accountability and care team was assembled from among the leadership of our church to partner with John and Joan in this process. Later, as it became clear that the restoration and recovery process would require John and Joan to relocate out of the area, another Spiritual Care Team was put together in the Northwest, near their new home, to more directly be a part of John and Joan's life.

Our guiding theme in developing our actions throughout this time was a commitment to what we saw as the balancing aspects of God's character. We recognized that, as the church, we were being watched not just by our people but by our community. We saw in this an opportunity to show that God's character is fully righteous and holy; God hates sin yet is also loving and gracious, loving the sinner and seeking repentance and restoration. Our primary teaching focus was understanding how we as a church body could respond strongly against sin, how we could protect the very precious office of the elder/overseer/chief undershepherd, and yet how we could respond to our repentant leader and friend in such a way as to clearly seek his restoration within the body.

From that time to the present, John and Joan have continued to willingly and actively place themselves in submission to and seek guidance, direction and accountability from both Spiritual Care Teams.

From early 1992 through the summer of 1994, John's restoration process was focused on (1) his spiritual restoration to God and (2) his restoration to the fellowship of believers at our church. This phase culminated in a church service on September 1, 1994, in which our church joined with John and Joan in a joyous celebration of God's grace and wondrous work in strongly moving ahead in both of these restoration steps.

This example is important in showing the concept and function of the Spiritual Care Team. It shows strong commitment to the restoration process carried out over an extended period of time. It shows concerned Christians unwilling to leave a job half-finished when relocation and physical distance could have interrupted it. It stands in sharp contrasGt to the "out of sight, out of mind" and "good riddance" points of view that we have seen are inadequate responses to the need for restoration.

The Rural Oregon Church

The next example of establishing a Spiritual Care Team is taken from a medium-sized church in rural Oregon. I have worked closely with this church and also have a counseling practice there.

The assistant pastor, Andy, discusses his experience in implementing the Spiritual Care Team concept in his church.

I had been counseling Darlene for some time regarding her present relationship with her parents. They had been vey abusive to her during her childhood. During her counseling, Darlene realized that she needed to tell her husband, David, about the abuse she had experienced as an adolescent. She realized that her abuse was having an impact on their marital relationship. David was so convicted by her transparency and her concern for the marriage that he later confessed a one-time sexual encounter with a coworker. This resulted in serious marital disruption.

After David confessed the affair, I worked with them individually and eventually together on restoring trust. Because broken trust was such a sensitive issue for Darlene, given her upbringing, she would frequently bring up a valid area of concern about her husband's behavior but then waver as to whether or not she had the right to hold him accountable. She felt that David was still being deceptive with his feelings and minimizing the amount of damage that his affair had caused the relationship, but she would invalidate her own right to express hurt or frustration over his actions. I felt that it would take a lot of pressure off their healing process if she could experience the support of some advocates who could help her interpret her husband's trustworthiness and find an appropriate response to his wrong behaviors by modeling correct biblical indignation and confrontation. So I discussed with them the concept of putting a Spiritual Care Team together to create these supportive relationships. They were willing to pursue this option.

After consulting my colleagues on the pastoral staff, I suggested the name of one couple to be included on the team. I asked Darlene and David to submit the names of two other couples, from which we would choose one. We asked them to choose couples (1) with whom they were comfortable sharing their situation, (2) whom they respected as spiritually mature enough to give truthful feedback, and (3) who were assertive enough to hold them accountable. We found that praying about which people to invite to participate in the team was a growth experience in itself. We all looked at spiritual maturity in a more intense way. Darlene and David became aware for the first time of how important spiritual community is and that some people are not mature enough or are unsuitable in some way to commit to such an intense process.

I talked with the care team couples just prior to our first meeting. I gave them a scriptural mandate for what they were about to do and a specific lesson on how to deal with the essential issues around rebuilding trust. Then we all met together as a group. For the first hour of the first meeting I directed the conversation to make sure that all necessary facts were out on the table and to help them achieve a solid foundation for their expectations of how the group should work.

I now make personal contact with team members each month to make an assessment of progress and fine-tune the process.

So how is it working or not working? When someone has lived a lie for an extended time, he has learned to cover things by deflecting the gaze of others from the truth through deception and charm. It took the group about five months before they realized that it was more important to confront the small half-truths in David's story than it was to talk Darlene out of her angry response. For a period of time it appeared that David was simply going to try to wait out the group in their accountability demands. No one else in his life had ever held his feet to the fire long enough to ensure that he dealt with problems.

When the care team became more insistent in their demands that he follow through with his commitments, he became increasingly indignant and began to tell Darlene in private that the group process was not effective because God had already forgiven him and digging up the past was only hindering them from getting on with their future. Darlene found herself in the hot seat and was temporarily irritated that she had trusted herself to a group that was supposed to shoulder the burden with her but appeared to be throwing everything back in her lap.

She reported these things to me, and I was able to help her see that her frustration was the result not of the group's failure but of her husband's ability to manipulate circumstances to validate his desire to avoid change. She agreed to stop buffering her husband from the group and to insist that if he was frustrated, he should work it out with the group directly. When he insisted on trying to deal with things inappropriately, she would bring the evidence to light before the group, thus thwarting his cover-up capabilities.

The group process became more profitable for Darlene and more frustrating for David. However, David has finally arrived at the conclusion that he has a number of misperceptions and that he cannot restore trust in his marriage without learning the process of accountability with the help of some spiritually insightful confrontation. I believe that he could not have made this connection without the feedback the Spiritual Care Team gave him.

I believe the concept of the Spiritual Care Team is a valid and workable approach to restoration, especially in the lives of those who have had a leadership role in the church. However, it is clear that success hinges upon the willing participation of the restoree. From the restoree's point of view, the process is so painful that success depends on the evidence of long-term commitment to him or her as an individual rather than just the process. The restoree wants to see the possibility of acceptance and restoration in the heartfelt concern expressed by the team.

The Portland Church

Almost three years after my own restoration process had begun, another Spiritual Care Team need surfaced in a church in the Portland area. Peter, one of the associate pastors, resigned after confessing to having committed adultery with a member of the congregation. The senior pastor, who had been at the church for about two years, asked Sandy and me for help in developing a Spiritual Care Team to meet the resigning pastor's request for restoration. Sandy and I were asked to lead the team, which consisted of four couples and a single woman. One of the other couples eventually assumed the leadership of the team and directed the process through the formal restoration period. The new leader had served as a liaison to the church board of elders from the beginning. The formal process culminated after about fourteen months in a formal report to the board of elders and the congregation.

The details about this process can be helpful to others who wish to begin a restoration team, but remember that these examples will have to be adapted to fit the needs of a particular situation.

The team leader reported that at the organizational meeting of the Spiritual Care Team the senior pastor read four key Scriptures and emphasized their importance in restoration. They served as the *charge* to the restoration team and the restoree.

Galatians 6:1-2: restoration and healing along with the essential attitudes of gentleness and humility.

2 Corinthians 2:5-11: the danger of isolation; Satan getting a foothold.

Hebrews 3:12-13: the deceitfulness of sin. We can help one another live in the light. We need the attitude of encouragement.

Hebrews 10:24-25; 12:12-14: the importance of finding positive ways to stimulate growth.

The *purposes* of this particular Spiritual Care Team were outlined as follows:

☐ Provide nurture, encouragement and support during the recovery process.

☐ Provide channels of communication for special needs that may arise.

☐ Be a mirror to help face issues squarely and honestly.

☐ Provide accountability in working through the issues identified.

☐ Make recommendations concerning the process and timing of reentry into ministry, whether pastoral ministry or any other capacity.

☐ Supply direction as new issues surface.

Peter, the fallen pastor, also shared his initial suggestions of changes to be addressed:

☐ Grow in my personal relationship with God.

☐ Be more discerning concerning appropriate and inappropriate levels of intimacy in relationships outside of marriage.

☐ Grow in honesty with God and God's people; gain awareness of self-protective or deceitful patterns.

☐ Deal with anger more constructively.

☐ Relate more warmly and openly to members of God's family.

Following a discussion of the role of team members, Sandy and I shared our own experiences and stressed the things that we had found most helpful from our Spiritual Care Team. Peter, his wife, Jill, and all of the team agreed to begin the process. We met monthly for the next fourteen months. In addition, the male members of the team spent time with Peter and the female members with Jill.

At the conclusion of the fourteen-month process, the Spiritual Care Team made a report to the church board of elders indicating that the purposes of the Spiritual Care Team had been fulfilled and that key issues had been satisfactorily addressed. After direct questioning of the team members, the restoree and his family, the board passed the following resolution:

> This board accepts the report of November 17, 1993, presented by the Spiritual Care Team of Peter Jones, including the assessment that Peter should be restored to full fellowship within the Christian church as a coworker and trustworthy brother in Christ. Further, we affirm that the Spiritual Care Team may determine when Peter can be released to serve in any formal capacity within the church. The elders will issue a statement of affirmation and restoration to ministry based on the recommendation of the Spiritual Care Team.

The resolution was shared with the entire church family, and the process was concluded.

Final Thoughts

These examples demonstrate a variety of challenging circumstances that a Spiritual Care Team may face. They show how the Spiritual Care Team should be responsive to the needs of the specific restoree and his or her family. In one case the goals of restoration were reached in a relatively short period of time; in another case the process has been slower and more frustrating; in the third case it has been successful but complicated by relocation and the restoree's serious health problem. There is no magic formula. Each Spiritual Care Team has to deal with what they find. The examples have in common the need for support, accountability, spiritual challenge and long-term commitment to restoration. The keys to successful implementation of the model are the willingness of the restoree and the intense involvement of the Spiritual Care Team members.

The model is not perfect, but it is a beginning. We believe it is worth applying and perfecting. The goal is that people's lives that teeter on the brink of destruction because of sinful choices may be brought back into restored relationship with our merciful God, who always says, "Come to me." Then restored relationships with spouse, children, friends and church can follow.

Appendix B

Principles Regarding
Sexual Addiction

*A*lthough the following material is presented in a question-and-answer format, no actual interview took place. Larry Paulson submitted written questions to Dr. McIvor. His responses are summarized here with his permission.

What is the first thing a person must do to deal with a sexual addiction?

The offender must first admit that he or she has a problem with how sexuality is experienced and expressed and must take responsibility and be accountable for the *choices* made.

How clear-cut must the personal responsibility be?

Very clear-cut. Statements like "It's an addiction" (implying that the person didn't actually choose to carry out the behavior) are rationalizations or thinking errors that are simply not acceptable. Also, the person is not allowed to hide behind the skirts of faith. Statements like "It must have been God's will that I do these things" or "I let my spiritual attention lapse" or "Satan stepped in and look what happened" cannot be accepted.

My response is "You chose to put your penis where it didn't belong. You chose to call the person. You chose to be with the person. You chose to withhold the truth that you did these things from your spouse, your spiritual leaders, your peers. Let's focus on the choices you made and how you justified them to yourself."

You've discussed responsibility. What about accountability?

The offender must seek out being held accountable for his offenses, legally, morally and spiritually. If he has not been reported, he must turn himself in to the proper authorities. If he has been reported for one offense but there have been twenty offenses, he must report all twenty offenses. And the reporting must be specific.

What do you mean by "report"? Who should be involved in hearing what the offender has done?

I feel reporting it to employers, coworkers, family members and church members has a tremendous healing effect and allows the offender to reconnect with reality. To do so directly confronts the cognitive "macro" (in computer analogy, a sort of signal that triggers a series of recurring words or operations) that secrecy is better than honesty.

What about withholding truth?

You need to be prepared for such comments as "My family has suffered enough—it is too embarrassing for my wife and children to lay out all this information to the parish" or "I can't tell my parents of this—it would kill them. And if they had a stroke, I'd sue you for poor judgment." There are many rationalizations or justifications for "lying by omission" (choosing not to reveal information about one's prior choices that might not be approved of). Examples include, among others, the following points which Earl Wilson developed during therapy.

1. What they don't know won't hurt them.

2. What they don't know won't hurt me.

3. I'll tell when the time is right.

4. Why tell? They won't know if I don't.

5. They don't need to know.

6. They won't understand.

7. It isn't important that they know.

8. If I tell, I'll just hurt people who don't need to be hurt.

9. They will just use my confession as fodder for gossip.

10. I've hurt enough already. I don't want to open up more.

11. I'll just tell the part of the truth that is necessary.

12. If I tell the whole truth I will lose control.

13. People won't be able to forgive me if they know the whole truth.

14. It's better to let this whole thing die down.

15. I don't want innocent people to get hurt more (like my family and friends).

It appears that you are saying that these offenders have difficulty taking responsibility for their actions. Is that correct?

Individuals who commit these offenses have a remarkable ability to disassociate from any negative components of their offenses. They report that they simply do not experience or compute any possible negative outcome. In this mode of mental processing, there are *no* deterrents to misbehaving. It is important to understand that since the behavior occurred (often repeatedly in a variety of contexts), no deterrents were in effect. With "religious" offenders, when asked "What about the notion God is omniscient, omnipresent and omnipotent?" their response is something like "I didn't think about God at the time." Then often there is a chuckle with the realization that "If God is those three things, then clearly it is God's will that I do the things I do . . . "

What about the victims? Is any thought given to them by the offender?

Such offenders cut off any concerns about empathy, or they

create in their own minds a series of misperceptions and misinter-
pretations that lead them to report that they believe the victim
initiated the misbehavior and must have enjoyed it. This report has
occurred even when the victim was crying, thrashing around and
trying to get away from the offender. An important part of treatment
is at least going through the motions of empathy training, listening
to what real victims say and then writing out what they feel their
victims felt at the moment of the offense and are feeling now.

*You indicated that writing out is important. Could you explain
how it might assist in therapeutic treatment?*

I require patients to keep a daily journal on full-sized lined
notebook paper in a loose-leaf binder, in which they must write a
minimum of one full page a day. They may write more as needed.
This journal becomes a key therapeutic tool because it is a
complete record of everything the person writes and everything
the person *doesn't* write. It is a wonderful way to document lying
by omission. It is also a wonderful way to reveal and identify
thinking errors. Specific written assignments are sometimes
given, but often it is the random musings that occur with bore-
dom or upsetness that reveal specific patterns of thinking.

Family and children often reveal very significant events that
the offender does *not* record in his journal, because "I didn't think
it was important enough to write about" (hit his refrigerator so
hard he left a two-inch dent in it, terrifying his wife and four
young children), or "I didn't think that's what you wanted me to
write about" (told a dirty joke to a fellow student, who was so upset
she went into the restroom, threw up, then quit her job).

*You have indicated that offenders misperceive and tend to
rationalize—and that they don't always see clearly how their
victims are impacted. Is it important that these offenders understand how their actions have affected others?*

Yes, offenders need to see how their misbehavior has affected
others around them. Finally noticing the pain they have brought

to people they care about can sometimes be the trigger for change.

I recall working with three daughters, ages fourteen, fifteen and sixteen, whose total school experiences were destroyed when their father's name and photo appeared in the local paper for sexual offense convictions. This father had given absolutely no thought to what impact his sexual escapades would have on his daughters' social lives.

Family finances are turned upside down as families watch finances drain away to lawyers and therapists. As I interview spouses of such offenders, the spouses often say in tears, "My life has been ruined. I have lost my home. My husband has lost his source of income. I have done nothing wrong, yet I have been punished." The majority of offenders give absolutely no thought to such matters when they are offending.

What response should the offender have to the victim?

I feel it is important for the offender to apologize in public to the victim. It is important to understand that when someone says "I am asking for your forgiveness," that is *not* an apology, but is simply more abuse and victimization. The victim does *not* have to forgive. The burden for the solution, since the problem was caused by the offender, lies with the offender.

Apologizing means saying, "I'm sorry I did _____, _____ and _____. I was wrong to do that. I hurt you and had no right or excuse to hurt you. I will never do that again to you or anyone else. I realize I was wrong to do that because _____, _____ and _____. I also understand that you are under no obligation to forgive me. I must make the corrective action. I am willing to pay for your treatment if you need treatment, and I am willing to do whatever you ask."

Anything less than this is phony, superficial and abusive. Many offenders will pressure or manipulate Christians into saying that they forgive the offender, because a Christian who does not forgive feels like a lousy Christian or a hypocrite. I feel it is *abusive* to put a Christian in this position, and I want the offender to spend some time doing empathetic thinking about how to make amends.

You have hinted that a person's Christian faith may be a hindrance in recovery. Can you explain that further?

Christians, by definition, are not reality-based. They may draw conclusions and make decisions by appeal to authority (Scripture; a religious leader), by revelation or by uncritical faith. Because the illogical is thus accepted, it is very easy for a sex offender to manipulate from within this system.

This is the primary reason most churches have allowed clergy-offenders to escape any legal consequences for their offenses for so many years. There is a sort of unspoken taboo among Christians not to critically evaluate any other Christian's faith. Thus, when an offender is caught and says, "I have fallen from grace, but thank God, and in Jesus' name, I am saved once again, and I will go and sin no more," what on earth are the church authorities to say? Most have no idea what to say. I have conducted support groups for clergy on these issues, and they have told me that they have received no training and have no reference material on these issues.

I have watched a youth pastor who had molested fifteen children in his own church escape the legal justice system because he personally went to the parents of each of the fifteen identified victims (not the other four who never told until later), apologized and asked for their forgiveness. Of the fifteen sets of parents, fourteen forgave him and would not press charges. One set of parents filed charges, but the offense was reduced to a misdemeanor because the minister was so "repentant." I believe this minister is still molesting children today. He never received any treatment. His attorney's secretary risked her job to call me and tell me in tears how wrong she felt her boss was to distort all parts of this pastor's reality to get him a light legal outcome.

My experience has shown me a man who had sexual intercourse

with all of his young children, had a jailhouse conversion, was given an extremely light sentence, joined a church, befriended a farming family in the church, got a job with them, got them to trust him and then sexually approached their high-school daughter. This family saw no problem in leaving their daughter alone with a convicted multiple sex offender because he was "born again."

Prison chapels are perfect places for passing and storing weapons, drugs and messages. The pattern seems to be that it is difficult to have spiritual faith and common sense! With an intelligent, verbally skilled offender, it is easy enough to present a convincing picture of remorse, repentance, spiritual renewal and a new direction. Such a pattern can fool anyone, but especially it seems to fool religious people. I do not feel good about these observations, as I am a minister's son and tend to be proreligious in broad terms. But I have seen too many offenders easily hide within the religious framework.

What about Christian churches? Are they any help in dealing with these matters or these types of offenses?

Generally, most churches have no resources or information to deal with this topic. It seems to be taboo in churches. My frustration with the church, and probably a reason I did not pursue training in the ministry, is that the church seems to have split itself off from the reality of daily life. When battered wives tell their ministers of their abuse, many ministers instruct them to submit to their husbands, turn the other cheek, forgive seventy times seven times, and pray. None of these suggestions help; in fact, they result in further abuse. Whole groups of ministers steer their flock away from mental health care. This is appalling to me!

It is difficult to be a minister or church leader. One must try to balance all the various cliques and pressure points in a parish. This is a complex art! In my fifteen years in one area, I have been called by five chaplains and two ministers. The two ministers were very helpful to their sexual-offender parishioners. They were supportive, kind, firm and fair. They were eager to learn, and I supplied them with as much information as possible. But generally my experience has been that most churches do not want to talk about such problems. I think this is tragic.

Is there hope? Can a person really recover from sexual addiction?

I reject the concept of sexual addiction because it implies that the person is not responsible for his own choices. The individuals who do these things make thousands of repetitive, complex, interacting decisions and choices all along the way, and they demonstrate by their own histories that they know exactly what they are doing, how far they can go, and what steps to take to avoid detection. The recidivism rate, I believe, hovers around 60-70 percent for those individuals who are not legally confronted, around 35 percent for those who are incarcerated and around 12 percent for those who receive skilled treatment. This is a sketchy estimate on my part. Most of the clergy that I have dealt with who have committed such offenses have committed many, many offenses, have been caught before, have had their hands slapped— and the whole matter was covered over.

I feel this is like covering over a spot of leprosy. Covering over is not effective. Our research is so new in this area that we don't yet have good longitudinal data. But people who work in this field talk of the "relapse prevention" model originally developed by Alan Marlatt, Ph.D., in dealing with alcoholism, and written about by D. Richard Laws in *Relapse Prevention with Sex Offenders* (New York: Guilford, 1989).

You know about our Spiritual Care Team and its work. What do you feel is the benefit of such a team?

The two most important functions of a Spiritual Care Team are:

1. The team should eliminate secrecy. The team members *must* know all the detailed facts. They need to be ever watchful for when

an offender begins to drift back into lying by omission or "gilding the lily" (putting a positive spin on some fraction of the truth). For example, when the offender says, "I've prayed a lot about that lately," be sure to inquire into the details. The person may have been napping, reading or watching TV and counting it as prayer time. Consider having him write out one of those long prayers. Beware of the common religious error: "He says he prayed for several hours, so he must have done so, because a Christian would never lie about such things." There are countless ways a spiritual team can pin down an offender's tendency to overemphasize the positive and omit the negative. I recommend that such teams go for verifiable details. Don't expect the offender to like this. In fact, most offenders who lie are quite offended when someone implies that they lie.

2. The spiritual support team can provide human emotional support. The team maintains friendship *and* sets appropriate limits. The dual message is: "We love you, we care for you, we will stick with you—*and* you need to do what we say. We care for you, but what you did is not acceptable." Unfortunately, very few offenders really get the message that their behavior is unacceptable until they have ridden in the back of a police car or served some lockup time. Rather, the complex and seldom spoken thought is "Hey, with the right attorney and the right words, I can beat any system . . ."

I feel the Spiritual Care Team can also be helpful in maintaining frequent contact with the offender, the spouse and the children. Many times, such offenders are not sensitive or empathetic toward their own families. The team can remind and reassure the spouse and children that they did not cause the offender to make his own complex and destructive choices.

Other functions the team can provide include assisting the family in finding appropriate resource people, seeing that the nonoffending spouse and children get support as needed, being alert to when the offender may be emotionally pushing or abusing his family, and helping the offender come forward in his church to publicly announce what he has done and take 100 percent responsibility for it. The team can also work closely with the offender's therapist and probation officer.

The main negative effect of such a team will occur if they tend to reframe the offense into spiritual dynamics or into a "spiritual problem." If this occurs, then it is quite simple for an offender to accommodate to such a reframe: just have a religious renewal experience, and then "the problem" will dissolve.

The other risk is that the Spiritual Care Team will join the offender in minimizing his offense. They may even collude with the offender against the legal justice system or the therapist, providing the offender with assistance in beating the legal justice system, going around the therapist's limits or assignments, or in other ways softening or sabotaging treatment. The greatest arena or focus for this to occur can be the religious or spiritual arena: "Well, the therapist is not washed in the blood of the same Lamb we are washed in, so we'll just humor her, and I think we can let the offender be alone with vulnerable clients again . . ." or "Doesn't the therapist seem to have drifted away from the spirit of Christ's presence? He doesn't pray before each session and ask for guidance (or, he doesn't attend our church, or, he doesn't attend any church), so he probably isn't the most spiritually appropriate therapist for our offender."

The above are complex issues that most offenders will be very skilled to mold toward their own benefit.

You place great emphasis on truth. Would you comment further on why you emphasize this, particularly for Christians?

Twelve-step programs and other groups identify it as an important issue. When someone in a stop-smoking group continues to smoke and tells the group they have not smoked, they are lying to the group and to themselves and are making the whole process a sham. These groups teach that it is important to be truthful. Weight-loss programs often have people weigh in. This is touching base with the truth.

Those who have committed sexual offenses tend to do so with a rich fabric of complex, carefully planned, well-chosen lies. These patterns must be confronted and broken. Each person needs to learn to live with and know the truth.

My experience with Christians and the truth has been dismal. It was what motivated me to drop out of the church in my student years. I saw large numbers of church folks (including myself) lie. When I went back to the church for my own reasons as a young adult, I was again astounded at the casual disregard for the truth in the church. I see this pattern continued into the present. At age fifty-four, however, I understand that this is not a special problem of the Christians. It seems to be part of being human. But it is so widespread among people who commit sexual offenses that even the *offenders* eventually begin to notice it in themselves—and especially in other offenders in group therapy.

I think the issue of truth transcends religious orientation. And telling the truth just seems to be almost impossible to do. I am not 100 percent truthful, and I do not expect my sexual offender clients to be 100 percent truthful. But when they are cheating on their wives, I feel they should tell them.